BEST DAMN DESSERTS
FROM BEAR WALLOW TO GOOSEHORN

Best Damn Desserts
from Bear Wallow
to Goosehorn

Delicious Southern Desserts and Delicacies

LaVece Hughes

WIND PUBLICATIONS
2005

International Standard Book Number 1893239470
Library of Congress Control Number 2005931652

First Edition

Also by LaVece Hughes:

Generations—A Dickinson Heritage Cookbook (1993)

Cooking With My Friends—Kentucky Recipes Tried and True (2003)

Foreword

Mealtime is is a time for more than eating the nutrients to keep your body alive and healthy. It is a time to be with friends and family, to share daily trials and tribulations, and discuss solutions to the world's problems. To me the best part of a meal is dessert, whether it is the culmination of a feast or the finale to a simple salad meal.

I come from a Southern family and have parents who grew up during the depression, but they never acted as if they were poor or disadvantaged. My mother always prepared well-thought-out meals, which made use of simple, reasonable groceries. She taught me to cook as I watched while she prepared meals. She would usually plan the dessert for a meal first, and then ask, "Now, what should we have to go with this dessert?"

This book is dedicated to all those, family members and friends, who have shared recipes with me. I have included recipes for the very best desserts that I have had the privilege to enjoy. These recipes include new, old, easy, and even a few complicated ones that I have collected over the years. I have worked to make them as simple as possible, substituting use of the microwave, and mixes when possible. I have also included a few sweet appetizers, breakfast breads, sweet salads that some consider desserts, and even some sweet fruits and vegetables.

As we say down home, "It's time to eat, y'all!"

— LaVece Ganter Hughes

Contents

Pies

Cakes

Cookies and Brownies

Pies

Granny Smith Apple Pie ... great

2 pie crusts rolled in sheets	¾ t cinnamon
6-7 Granny Smith apples, chopped	¼ t nutmeg
¾ c sugar	1 T lemon juice
3 T flour	2 T butter

Place one of the pie crust sheets in the pie pan. Unroll the 2nd crust. Combine sugar, flour, cinnamon, nutmeg in a large bowl. Toss well to mix. Add lemon juice over the apples, and stir. Pour apples into flour mixture and mix gently.

Pour apples into pie crust. Dot the fruit with butter. Dampen the top crust with water. Invert the top pastry over the filling, center and slowly peel off the paper, pressing down along the edge to seal. Sculpt the overhanging dough into an upstanding ridge. Sprinkle the top of the pie generously with sugar. Poke steam vents in the pie. Bake in a 375 degree oven for 50-55 minutes. Serve warm or at room temperature.

Apple Chess Pie

7 T butter or margarine	2 eggs, beaten
1 c sugar	unbaked pie shell
1 t flour	1 c tart apples, cut in small pieces
dash of cinnamon	

Melt butter, add flour, sugar and cinnamon. Add eggs and apples. Mix and pour into unbaked pie shell. Bake at 375 degrees for 15 minutes. Reduce heat to 350 degrees and bake for 30 more minutes.

Apple Crisp

2 c sugar	1 t soda
½ c butter	1 t salt
2 eggs	2 c flour
1 t cinnamon	4 c apples, chopped
1 t nutmeg	

Cream sugar and butter. Beat in eggs. Sift dry ingredients and add to egg mixture. Stir in apples. Pour into greased pyrex baking dish. Bake one hour at 350 degrees. Serve with Kool Whip or ice cream.

Apple Peanut Butter Crisp

6-8 green apples, pared and sliced   ¾ c flour
½ c water   ¾ c brown sugar
2 T lemon juice   ⅓ c peanut butter
1 T cinnamon   ¼ c margarine

Preheat oven to 350 degrees. Arrange apple slices in bottom of a lightly oiled 9 x 13 inch baking pan. Mix lemon juice and water and pour over apples. Sprinkle cinnamon on top. Mix remaining ingredients until crumbly. Spread evenly over the apples. Bake for about 40 minutes, or until golden brown. Serve with ice cream or a dollop of kool whip.

Apple Cream Pie

4 c sliced peeled tart apples   1 c whipping cream
9 inch unbaked pastry shell   3 T flour
1 c sugar   cinnamon

Place apples in pie shell. Combine sugar, cream and flour. Pour over the apples. Sprinkle with cinnamon. Bake at 400 degrees for 10 minutes. Reduce heat to 375 degrees; bake for 35-40 minutes or until pie is set in center. Cover crust edges with foil during the last 15 minutes if needed. Cool on a wire rack. Serves 6-8.

Best Ever Apple Dumplings

Pie Crust: *Vanilla Sauce:*
1 c flour   1 c sugar
2 T shortening, heaping   1 T flour
3 T water   2 c water
(Or use prepared crust)   *Stir and bring to a boil.*
                                         Add:
Mix and roll out for   1 t vanilla
dumplings.   1 T butter

Use 3 medium apples, slice thin and put in bowl, sprinkle with sugar, 1 T flour and a little nutmeg. Place on pastry squares. Add 4 cinnamon red hots to each.   Pinch together. Put in an 8 x 8 pan and bake at 400 degrees. As soon as they are in the oven make sauce. By the time it boils, dumplings should be starting to brown on top. Pour thin sauce over dumplings and continue baking until done. Sauce will have cooked up quite a bit. Serve with ice cream or whipped cream.

The Best Apple Stuff, Ever!

4 apples, peeled and sliced thin
1½ c water (pour over apples)
½ c sugar (sprinkle on top)

1 dry white or yellow cake mix
1½ sticks melted margarine
cinnamon (sift on top)
1 c chopped pecans or almonds

Spray a 9 x 13 baking dish with Pam and layer ingredients in the order listed. Bake at 375 degrees for 45 minutes. Serve warm or cold.

Baked Apple Dumplings

pastry sheets (available in
   freezer section of grocery)
Granny Smith apples

cinnamon sticks for each apple
1 jar apricot preserves
brown sugar

Thaw and unfold pastry sheets. Core and peel Granny Smith apples and place each in center of a sheet of puff pastry, trimming to make a circle. Insert a cinnamon stick in hollow; spoon in 1 teaspoon apricot preserves, 1 tablespoon brown sugar. Lightly brush exposed pastry with water. Repeat with remaining apples. Fold up pastry, smoothing over apple, pressing folds to seal and gathering corners at top. Trim excess. Brush each dumpling with milk and sprinkle with granulated sugar. Bake in a 350-degree oven for 30-35 minutes until pastry is golden brown.

Berry Apple Pie

1 c sugar
1 t quick cooking tapioca
½ t cinnamon
2 prepared crusts, uncooked

2 c blackberries or blueberries
2 c sliced, peeled apples
2 T butter, cut up

Mix and let sit for 15 minutes. Pour into 9½-inch pie pan lined with piecrust. Cover with second crust. Sprinkle with sugar. Cook for 25 minutes in a 375-degree oven.

"The next time you feel like complaining, remember that your garbage disposal probably eats better than 30 percent of the people in the world."
— Robert Orben

Fried Apple Pies

Crust:	Filling:
2 c plain flour	3 medium sweet apples, peeled
1 t salt	and chopped
2 t baking powder	1 T water
¼ t soda	⅔ c sugar
3 T shortening	1 T flour
buttermilk*	¼ t cinnamon
	¼ t nutmeg

To make filling:
Combine apples and water in saucepan. Cover and cook on low heat until tender, approximately 10-15 minutes. Drain liquid. Combine sugar, flour and spices and stir well. Add to apples. Cook until thickened, about 10 minutes.

To make crust:
Sift flour, salt, baking powder and soda together. Cut in shortening. Add enough buttermilk to moisten. Knead on floured board until smooth. Roll out very thin and cut around the shape of a cereal bowl to make pies.

To assemble pies:
Add 2 tablespoons of filling to a crust; fold over and crimp edges with a fork dipped in water to seal edges. Heat oil in a cast iron skillet and fry until brown on one side, and then flip and brown the other side. Drain on paper towels and sprinkle with sugar.

Optional: May place uncooked pies on a baking sheet spayed with Pam, sprinkle with sugar and bake in a 350 degree oven for 20 minutes, or until pies begin to brown.

* Old time cooks would combine 2 tablespoons of vinegar with ½ cup milk and let sit until thickened for a buttermilk substitute.

"This recipe is certainly silly. It says to separate two eggs, but it doesn't say how far to separate them."
— Gracie Allen

Banana Pudding Supreme

8 oz cream cheese
1 c sweetened condensed milk
1 c cold milk
3.4 oz pkg instant vanilla pudding

8 oz Kool Whip, thawed
55 vanilla wafers
4 medium banana

In a mixing bowl beat cream cheese until smooth. Beat in condensed milk and set aside. In another bowl, whisk milk and pudding mix. Add to cream cheese mixture. Fold in Kool Whip. Place a third of vanilla wafers in a 2 ½ quart bowl. Top with a third of the sliced bananas and pudding mixture. Repeat layers twice. Refrigerate until serving.

Virgil's Nutty Banana Pudding

2 pkgs cook-and-serve banana
   cream pie filling
2 T vanilla
2 bananas

1 c nuts, chopped
   vanilla wafers
Kool Whip
1 c shredded coconut

Cook banana cream pie filling (follow pudding directions); add vanilla and add bananas (split horizontally and vertically then slice so the chunks of banana will be small); add nuts, (coarsely chopped pecans, walnuts or combination); Layer vanilla wafers on bottom of pan or dish and add pudding mix; after cooling, top with mixture of Kool Whip and coconut, then sprinkle coconut on top.

"I love nuts of all kinds and probably include what others might consider excessive amounts." — Virgil.

Blackberry Camp Meeting Pie … Good and Easy

1 stick butter
1 c flour
1 c sugar

1 t baking powder
1 qt blackberries or other fruit

Melt butter in a 13 x 9 inch dish in the oven. Mix flour, sugar and baking powder in a bowl. Pour batter over the melted butter. Do not stir. Heat fruit and pour on top of butter/batter mixture. Do not stir. Bake at 350 degrees for 30 minutes or until golden brown on top.

Blackberry Cobbler … an oldie, but goodie

Crust:
3 cups flour
12 T shortening
6 T water

Cobbler:
2 qt blackberries
3 c sugar
3 T flour
½ c water
4 T butter

Put blackberries in large pan. Pour the 3 T flour, 3 cups sugar, and ½ cup water over berries, gently stirring to mix in flour. While preparing crust, heat berries just to a boil on medium high heat.

In mixing bowl, cut shortening into flour and add water. Mix dough thoroughly. Flour wax paper and roll dough out between two pieces into a rectangle about 12 x 20 inches. Use extra flour to prevent crust from sticking to wax paper. Remove wax paper from one side of crust and turn over into the bottom corner of a 13 x 9 inch Pyrex dish, leaving the rest of the crust hanging over the edge of the other side.

After berries have just come to a boil, pour them into the dish and dot with about 4 T butter. Flip the rest of the crust over the top of the berries and tuck into the opposite side. Sprinkle sugar over the top. Bake for 35 minutes at 375 degrees.

This is the "old time" way of making blackberry cobbler passed down from my grandmother. It makes lots of juice. My kids love it with ice cream.

Blackberry Cobbler

2 c fresh blackberries (or can)
1 c flour
½ c sugar
1 t baking powder

1 stick butter, melted
½ c milk
½ t vanilla
½ c hot water
½ c sugar

Preheat oven to 350 degrees. Place blackberries in a 9 x 9 pan. Combine butter, flour, ½ c sugar, baking powder, milk and vanilla. Pour over fruit. Combine water and ½ c sugar. Pour over flour mixture. Bake for 55 minutes or till done.

Be kind to your kids - They chose your nursing home.
— Bumper sticker

Fruit Cobbler ... for your favorite fruit

Batter:
1 c self-rising flour
½ c sugar
½ c milk

Fruit:
3 c fresh fruit(or 15 oz can)
1 c sugar
2 T flour
7 T butter or margarine

Preheat oven to 350 degrees. Melt butter in 9 x 13 inch baking dish. Toss together fruit, sugar and flour. Pour batter into baking dish. Spoon fruit mixture over the top. Bake 30-40 minutes or until the batter is golden and the fruit is bubbly. Serve warm with ice cream.

Can thicken the cobbler by adding ½ cup more flour to the batter. For a more cake-like cobbler double the batter recipe.

Quick Cherry Crisp

1 can cherry pie filling
¼ c margarine

Jiffy Cake Mix (or 1 c cake mix)
½ c chopped nuts (optional)

Butter a 9-inch square Pyrex dish. Pour 1 can cherry pie filling into dish. Mix margarine with cake mix. Sprinkle cake mixture over filling. Bake at 350 degrees for 45-50 minutes.

Blueberry Surprise

1 stick margarine, melted
1 c flour

¼ c brown sugar
1 c nuts, chopped

Mix all together and press into a 9 x 12 inch pan. Bake for 15 minutes at 350 degrees. Cool completely. Then mix:

1 c sugar
8 oz Kool Whip

8 oz cream cheese
1 t vanilla

Spread onto cooled crust and top with a can of blueberry pie filling (cherry or other flavors can be used as well.) Refrigerate at least one hour.

Some say the glass is half empty; some say the glass is half full,
I say, are you going to drink that?
— Lisa Claymen

Blueberry Blitz

1 c flour
½ c chopped pecans
1 stick butter
¼ c brown sugar

1 can blueberry pie filling
8 oz cream cheese softened
¾ c sugar
1 c Kool Whip, thawed

Cream butter and sugar until fluffy. Add flour and pecans and mix well. Spray a 9 x 13 pan with vegetable oil. Press the pecan mixture in bottom of pan and slightly up the sides. Bake at 325 degrees for 15—20 minutes until lightly browned. Cool. Beat cream cheese until fluffy. Gradually beat in sugar. Fold in Kool Whip. Spread mixture over crust. Spread blueberry pie filling over cream cheese mixture. Cover and chill until firm.

Buttermilk Pie

2 c sugar
5 T flour
½ c melted butter
3 eggs

1 t vanilla
1 c buttermilk
1 unbaked pie shell

Mix well and pour into unbaked pie shell. Cook at 350 degrees for 45 minutes.

Cherry Pie … 5 minute preparation

15-oz pkg prepared refrigerated pie crusts
1 can cherry pie filling

Place one crust in bottom of a 9-inch pie pan. Pour in a can of pie filling. Cut second crust into strips. Alternate strips vertically and horizontally over the pie. Crimp edges with a fork. Sprinkle sugar on top and cook for 30 minutes at 350 degrees until browned.

"Never eat more than you can lift"
— Miss Piggy.

Jeanne's Flaky Pie Crust ... really good and crisp

1 stick butter, softened   1 c flour
3 oz cream cheese

Heat oven to 450 degrees. Combine butter, cream cheese, and flour in small bowl. Mix until dough forms a ball and cleans the bowl; dough will be puffy and soft. Pat dough with floured hands into 9-inch pie pan, bringing up dough to edge of pan. If you like, flute edge. Score bottom and side with a fork. Add filling and bake according to directions, or bake 8-10 minutes for a baked pie shell. Cool

So-Easy Cherry Cobbler

2 20-oz cans cherry pie filling   5 white bread slices
15-oz can pitted, dark, sweet   1¼ c sugar
   cherries in heavy syrup, drained ½ c butter or margarine, melted
¼ c flour, divided   1 large egg
½ t almond extract   1½ t grated lemon rind

Stir together pie filing, cherries and 2 tablespoons flour. Stir in almond extract. Place in a lightly greased 8 inch square baking dish. Trim crusts from bread slices; cut each slice into 5 strips. Arrange bread strips over fruit mixture. Stir together remaining 2 tablespoons of flour, sugar, butter, egg and lemon rind; drizzle over bread strips. Bake at 350 degrees for 35-45 minutes or until golden and bubbly.

So-Easy peach cobbler— substitute frozen peaches, thawed, for cherries. Omit almond extract and lemon rind. *Too-easy berry cobbler*— substitute a can of blueberry pie filling and 20 oz frozen whole strawberries, unthawed, for cherries. Omit almond extract, and add 1 teaspoon vanilla and 1 teaspoon lemon juice.

Chess Pie ... a good old family recipe

½ c margarine   ½ c egg yolks (6)
2 c sugar   1 T flour
1 T corn meal   1 T vanilla
1 can of Pet milk   1 unbaked pie crust

Combine and pour into an unbaked pie shell. Bake for 15 minutes at 375 degrees, and then turn down the oven to 325 degrees for 30 minutes until lightly browned.

Butterscotch Pie

Beat: 3 egg yolks
Add: 2 cups milk

Combine and add to above:
1 c brown sugar
6 scant T flour
½ t salt
Cook on medium heat until thick,
stirring constantly. Cook until it
begins to bubble and thickens.

Then add:
4 T butter
1 t vanilla
1 or 2 T fresh brown sugar

Pour into baked pie shell.
Top with meringue, and bake
in 350 degree oven until
browned.

Meringue:
Beat 3 egg whites in glass mixing bowl until soft peaks form. Add 1 t
vanilla and 6 T of sugar gradually, beating until stiff peaks form. Spread
over pie, sealing to edge, and bake in a 350 degree oven for 15 minutes or
until lightly brown.

*Take care not to have any egg yolk in egg whites as whites will not beat
up into stiff peaks if there is any yellow in them.*

Chocolate Pie ... yummy and never fails

3 egg yolks, beaten
1½ c sugar
¼ c flour
2 T butter
2 heaping T cocoa

1 t vanilla
1¾ c evaporated milk
1 baked 9-inch pie shell
3 egg whites
6 T sugar

Place egg yolks, and sifted 1½ cup sugar and flour into a saucepan. Stir in
butter, cocoa, vanilla and evaporated milk. Cook over medium heat until
thickened, stirring constantly. Pour into pie shell. Beat egg whites in glass
mixing bowl until soft peaks form. Add vanilla and 6 T of sugar gradually,
beating until stiff peaks form. Spread over pie, sealing to edge and bake in
a 325 degree oven for 15 minutes or until lightly brown.
Always a great chocolate pie.

How much butter is that?
1 stick of butter = 7½ tablespoons = almost a half cup (8 oz)

Liz's Microwave Chocolate Pie ...yummy

1 c sugar	2 egg yolks, slightly beaten, and
3 T cocoa	separated
4 T cornstarch	1 t vanilla or almond extract
2 c milk	2 T butter
	1 baked pie shell, cooled

Mix together thoroughly and microwave sugar, cocoa, cornstarch, and milk on high for 3-4 minutes. Stir! Microwave 3 more minutes. Stirring until mixture is smooth, thickened and clear.

Stir a small amount of hot pudding quickly into egg yolks. Return egg mixture to hot pudding, mixing well. Microwave at medium high heat for 1 to 3 minutes, stirring after 1 minute, until smooth and thickened.

Add butter and vanilla. Stir until butter is melted. Pour into baked pie shell. Add meringue and bake until browned.

Meringue:
Beat 3 egg whites until frothy. Add 6 T sugar and ½ t cream of tartar. Beat with mixer until soft peaks form. Pour on top of hot pie filling and spread evenly to edges of crust. Bake at 350 degrees oven until meringue begins to brown, about 20 minutes.

Mile-High Meringue

7 large egg whites	¾ c sugar
½ t cream of tartar	1 t vanilla
pinch of salt	

Beat egg whites with mixer going from med to high. Add cream of tartar, and a pinch of salt. As egg whites get frothy add sugar little by little. Add 1 tsp vanilla. Beat until stiff. Cover entire pie with meringue making sure to secure edges. Bake at 375 degrees for 8-10 min. Cool two to three hours.

Be sure and lower the top rack of your oven to be able to brown the mile high meringue and not chop off the top.

"There are four basic food groups, milk chocolate, dark chocolate, white chocolate, and chocolate truffles."
— Unknown

4-Layer Chocolate Dessert … a family favorite

First layer:

1½ c flour   ½ c chopped pecans
1¼ stick butter (10 T)

Mix and pat into 9 x 13 inch Pyrex pan. Cook for 20 minutes in a 375 degrees oven. Cool

Second Layer:

8 oz cream cheese   ½ large carton Kool Whip
1 c powdered sugar   optional: (¼ c peanut butter)

Mix and pour over cooled crust.

Third Layer:

2 small boxes instant chocolate pudding *
3 cups milk
Spread pudding over 2nd layer

Fourth Layer:

Spread remaining Kool Whip and sprinkle with chopped pecans.

* Our family prefers chocolate pudding, but other flavors of pudding may be substituted.

Coconut Cream Pie

10-inch pie: *9-inch pie:*

1½ c sugar   1 c sugar
2 ½ T melted butter   2 T butter
3 eggs   2 eggs
1½ c sweet milk   1 c milk
2 c fresh grated coconut (or   1½ c coconut
    1 pkg frozen, grated)   1 t vanilla
1 t vanilla   dash salt
dash salt

Cream butter and sugar together. Then add eggs, one at a time while mixing. About 1 T of milk will mike it cream better. Mix in milk slowly and add vanilla and coconut. Pour into uncooked pie shell. Bake at 400 degrees for 10 minutes; then at 375 for 20 to 25 minutes until custard part of pie is set and top is browned. If pie is browning too fast, turn oven down to 350 degrees to finish baking.

Chocolate Peanut Butter Pie

1 chocolate crust pie shell

Chocolate Filling:
1⅓ c chocolate chips
¾ c mini-marshmallows
½ c low-fat sweetened condensed milk
¼ t vanilla
¾ c heavy cream

Peanut Butter Filling:
½ c low-fat sweetened
    condensed milk
½ c crunchy peanut butter
1½ c Kool whip, divided

Chocolate filling: In a medium saucepan over low heat, stir chocolate chips, marshmallows and milk until smooth. Transfer mixture to a bowl, stir in vanilla and let cool. Beat in heavy cream with an electric mixer until blended. Refrigerate 1 hour.

Peanut butter filling: In a medium saucepan over low heat, melt milk and peanut butter, mixing well. Let cool. Fold 1 cup of the Kool whip into the peanut butter mixture, then spread evenly into crust. Refrigerate until set.

Beat chocolate filling with an electric mixer on high until almost stiff. Spread over peanut butter layer, wrap and refrigerate 3 hours. Serve with Kool Whip. Serves 8.

Cranberry Walnut Pie … very good

1 shortbread pie crust
¾ c chopped walnuts
2 cans apple pie filling
¼ t nutmeg
1 6-oz bag sweetened dried cranberries
⅓ c flour
¼ c brown sugar, packed
3 T butter, melted

Heat oven to 375 degrees. Mix apple pie filling, cranberries and nutmeg. Spoon into crust. Combine flour and sugar; cut in butter until crumbly. Stir in walnuts; sprinkle over filing. Bake 35-45 minutes or until topping is browned.

Chocolate Pecan Ice Cream Torte ... delicious

1 jar caramel ice cream topping
2 1½-oz milk-chocolate candy
   bars, chopped
12 pecan sandies cookies, crushed
3 T butter, melted

1 c pecan halves, toasted, divided
½ gallon butter pecan ice cream,
   slightly softened
½ gallon chocolate ice cream,
   slightly softened

In a microwave-safe bowl, combine the caramel topping and candy bars. Microwave, uncovered, on high for 1 ½ minutes or until candy bars are melted, stirring every 30 seconds. Cool.

Combine the cookie crumbs and butter. Press onto the bottom of a greased 10 inch spring form pan. Chop ½ cup pecans; set aside. Spoon half of the butter pecan ice cream over crust. Drizzle with 2 tablespoon caramel sauce; sprinkle with ¼ cup chopped pecans. Spread half of the chocolate ice cream over top. Drizzle with 2 tablespoons caramel sauce; sprinkle with remaining chopped pecans. Spoon remaining butter pecan ice cream around the edge of pan; spread remaining chocolate ice cream in center of pan. Cover and freeze overnight. Carefully run a knife around edge of pan to loosen; remove sides of pan. Stick remaining pecan halves in top at 45 degree angles; drizzle with 2 tablespoons caramel sauce. Serve with remaining caramel sauce. Makes 20 servings.

French Silk Pie

¾ c sugar
¾ c butter
1 cup chocolate chips, melted and
   cooled

1 t vanilla
¾ c refrigerated or frozen egg
   product, thawed
1 baked pie shell

Prepare baked pie shell, and set aside. For filling, in a large mixing bowl beat sugar and butter with an electric mixer on medium speed about 4 minutes or until fluffy. Sir in chocolate chips melted and cooled and vanilla. Gradually add egg product, thawed, beating on high speed and scraping sides of bowl constantly till light and fluffy.

Transfer filling to baked pie shell. Cover and chill for 5-24 hours. Garnish with Kool Whip and chocolate curls Serves 10.

Crimson Pie

½ small orange, unpeeled, cut into pieces and seeded
4 c blueberries
3 c fresh or canned(drained) sour red cherries

1½ c sugar
3 T cornstarch
2 9 in pie crusts
2 T unsalted butter
milk to brush pastry

Coarsely grind orange in food processor. Transfer to medium saucepan. Add blueberries, cherries, sugar and cornstarch. Stirring constantly, bring mixture to a boil over high heat; cook until thick, about 3 minutes. Cool completely. Position the rack in the center of the oven; heat the oven to 400 degrees.

Fit one of the pie pastries in the bottom of a 9 inch pie pan. Spoon filling into pie crust, mounding it in the center. Dot filling with butter. Top with second pie crust. Trim, seal edges and crimp edge for decorative border. Make several slashes in top crust to allow steam; to escape. Brush crust with the milk. Sprinkle pie top with a little extra sugar. Place pie pan on rimmed cookie sheet. Bake until crust is golden brown, about 50 minutes. Cool on rack for 1 hour. Serves 8.

Kentucky Chocolate Nut Pie

1 c sugar
½ c flour
2 eggs, lightly beaten
½ c butter, softened
1 c chocolate chips

1 t vanilla
1 c chopped pecans
1 9-inch pie crust, unbaked

Bake crust for 10 minutes at 350 degrees. Remove and reduce oven temperature to 325 degrees. Mix sugar and flour together. Add eggs and butter. Stir in remaining ingredients and mix well. Pour filling into the partially baked pie shell. Bake at 325 degrees for 50-60 minutes until lightly browned.

This is the traditional pie named for the Kentucky Derby. Kerns Kitchens owns the name of "Derby Pie", and has sued to maintain that name, so others have to use their imaginations for their pie's names like First "Saturday in May" Pie or "Run for the Roses" Pie.

Ice Cream Sandwich Dessert

19 ice cream sandwiches
12 oz Kool Whip, thawed

12 oz hot fudge topping
1 c salted peanuts

Cut one ice cream sandwich in half. Place one whole and one half sandwich along a short side of an un-greased 13 x 9 pan. Arrange eight sandwiches in opposite direction in the pan. Spread with half of the whipped topping. Spoon ½ of the fudge topping by teaspoonfuls onto whipped topping. Sprinkle with ½ cup peanuts. Repeat layers with remaining ice cream sandwiches, whipped topping and peanuts (pan will be full). Cover and freeze for up to 2 months. Remove from the freezer 20 minutes before serving. Cut into squares. Serves 12-15.

"My family loves this dessert and it can be made, frozen, and then brought out months later. You can't tell it is made from ice cream sandwiches.

Triple-Layer … Easy Lemon Pie

2 c cold milk
2 pkg small Jell-O lemon instant
   pie filling*

1 graham cracker pie crust
8 oz Kool Whip

Pour milk into large bowl. Add dry pudding mixes. Beat with wire whisk until blended about 2 minutes. Spread 1½ cups of the pudding onto the bottom of the crust. Gently stir half of the Kool Whip into remaining pudding; spread over pudding layer in crust. Top with remaining Kool Whip. Refrigerate 3 hours. Serves 8.
* Can substitute chocolate, butterscotch or your favorite pudding.

Lemonade Pie

6-oz can frozen lemonade, thawed
1 can Eagle Brand Milk
12-oz container Kool Whip

29-oz can crushed pineapple, drained
3 oz Philadelphia cream cheese,
   softened
Graham cracker pie shell

Mix ingredients together and pour into a graham cracker crust. Chill overnight.

"The only two things I don't eat for breakfast are lunch and supper."
— Larry Holman

The Jello Story

Just married and still in college in the early 1960s, my husband and I were forced to find unusual and creative ways to stretch our budget. One ploy was to visit our respective parents on alternate weekends, always managing to tactfully hint at, and graciously accept, their gifts of a few groceries with which we stocked the meager shelves of our apartment's tiny kitchen.

One evening we were visited by Bart and his girlfriend Suetta. Bart is my cousin, and I'd introduced him to Suetta, one of my best college friends. They later married and have remained close friends and relatives for years. After a brief conversation, I went to the kitchen to prepare some refreshment. I had in mind Kool Aid for a beverage; it fit our budget. But I found the cupboard bare, no Kool Aid, no soft drinks, not even a single teabag.

Full of the resourcefulness of a newlywed, and proud of it, I had a flash of inspiration. I dissolved a package of cherry Jello in water, added sugar, and poured it over ice. Surprisingly, it easily passed my taste test. I served it to our guests and they seemed to enjoy it. But I did warn them to "drink it quickly."

Lemon Cream Pie

1½ c sugar
⅓ c plus 1 T cornstarch
1½ c cold water
3 egg yolks, lightly beaten
3 T butter, cubed
2 t grated lemon peel
½ c lemon juice

Crust:
1 c flour
1 c finely chopped walnuts
½ c cold butter

Topping:
8 oz cream cheese, softened
1 c powdered sugar
2 c cold milk
2 large pkgs instant vanilla
   pudding mix
1 t vanilla
16 oz Kool Whip, thawed

In a small saucepan, combine sugar and cornstarch; gradually stir in water until smooth. Bring to boil; cook and stir for 1 minute or until thickened. Remove from the heat. Stir a small amount of hot filing into egg yolks; return all to the pan, stirring constantly. Bring to a gentle boil; cook and stir for 1 minute. Remove from the heat; stir in butter and lemon peel. Gently stir in lemon juice. Refrigerate until cool.

In a bowl, combine flour and nuts. Cut in butter until mixture resembles coarse crumbs. Press into the bottom of a greased 13 in x 9 in x 2 in baking dish. Bake at 350 for 15-20 minutes or until edges are golden brown. Cool on a wire rack.

In a mixing bowl, beat cream cheese and powdered sugar until smooth; carefully spread over crust. Spread with cooled lemon mixture. In another mixing bowl, beat milk and pudding mixes on low for 2 minutes; beat in vanilla. Fold in half of the Kool whip. Spread over lemon layer. Spread with remaining Kool whip. Chill for at least 4 hours before serving. Yield:18-24.

"Other things are just food. But chocolate's chocolate."
— Patrick Skene Catling

Lemon Chess Pie ... an old family recipe

4 eggs
2 c sugar
1 T grated lemon rind
¼ c lemon juice
¼ c butter, melted

1 T cornmeal
1 T flour
¼ c milk
pinch salt
1 uncooked pie shell

Beat eggs; gradually add sugar. Stir in remaining ingredients. Pour into unbaked pie shell. Bake 350 degrees for 45-50 minutes or until brown. Do not over bake.

Lemon Lush Dessert

1 stick butter, melted
1 c flour
½ c nuts, finely chopped
1 c plus 1 T powdered sugar
1 large Kool Whip

8 oz cream cheese, softened
2 small pkgs. Lemon instant pudding
3 c milk
nuts, chopped

Mix margarine, flour and ½ cup chopped nuts and one tablespoon of powdered sugar. Pat into bottom of a 9 x 13 inch pan and bake 15 minutes at 350 degrees until lightly browned. Let cool.

Mix remaining powdered sugar, half the Kool Whip and cream cheese. Spread lightly over crust. Mix pudding and milk for two minutes on low speed. Spread over other layers. Spread remaining topping over top and sprinkle with nuts. Refrigerate four hours before serving.

Creamy Lemon Pie

1¾ c cold milk
1 6-oz can frozen lemonade
   concentrate, thawed

2 4-oz boxes vanilla instant pudding
1 8-oz Kool Whip, thawed
2 6-oz graham cracker crusts

Pour milk in large bowl, adding pudding mix, and beat 30 seconds. Add lemonade and beat 30 seconds more. Mix in Kool Whip and pour into crusts. Refrigerate 4 hours.

Sour Cream Lemon Pie ... wow, really good!

1 9-inch baked pie crust	zest of a lemon
¾ c sugar	3 T butter
3 T cornstarch	1 c sour cream
1 c milk	3 T sugar
3 eggs, separated	⅜ t cream of tartar
juice of 2 lemons	1 t vanilla

Combine ¾ cup of sugar, cornstarch, milk, and egg yolks in saucepan and cook over medium heat until very thick. Add lemon juice and some zest. Add butter and sour cream. Pour into the baked piecrust and top with meringue or Kool Whip.

Meringue:
Beat 3 egg white until frothy. Add 3 T sugar and ½ t cream of tartar. Beat until soft peaks form. Pour on top of hot pie filling and spread evenly to edges of crust. Bake at 350 degrees oven until meringue begins to brown; about 20 minutes.

Lemon Pie with Meringue Crust ... unique

Crust:

3 jumbo egg whites at room temperature	Add sugar and cream of tartar gradually to egg whites and beat until meringue forms stiff peaks. Spread into 2 large buttered pie plates. Bake at 300 degrees for 1 hour. Cool on rack.
¼ t cream of tartar	
1 c sugar	

Filling:

2 small pkgs cook-and-serve lemon pie filling	Cook pudding according to directions on boxes. Cool. Stir in 8 oz of Kool Whip. Spread filling evenly in pie shells then spread rest of Kool Whip on top of pies.
16 oz Kool Whip, thawed	

If you live to be a hundred, I want to live to be a 100, minus 1 day, so that I won' t have to live without you.
—*Winnie the Pooh*

Lemon Delight Dessert

1 stick butter
1 c self-rising flour
8 oz cream cheese
1 c powdered sugar

2 c Kool Whip
2 boxes lemon instant pudding
3 c milk

Melt butter; combine with flour and press into an 13 x 9 Pyrex pan and bake in a 400-degree oven until golden brown about 15 minutes. Cool. Mix cream cheese, powdered sugar and one cup of Kool Whip. Spread onto cooled crust. Mix pudding and milk and spread over cream cheese mixture. Spread remaining Kool Whip over top and keep refrigerated

Lemon Meringue Pie ... the old way

4 eggs
½ c sugar
3 T flour
3 T cornstarch
1½ c water

2 T margarine
1½ t grated lemon peel
⅓ c lemon juice
1 cooked pie shell

Mix sugar, flour, cornstarch and dash of salt. Gradually stir in water over medium heat until thickened and bubbly. Reduce heat and cook 2 minutes more. Remove from heat; slightly beat egg yolks. Gradually stir in 1 cup of hot filling into yolks. Pour into rest of mixture. Bring to gentle boil. Cook and stir 2 minutes more. Remove from heat and stir in margarine and lemon zest peel. Stir in lemon juice and pour into a cooked pie shell. Top with meringue and bake for 15 minutes at 350 degrees.

Perfect Meringue

3 egg whites
1 T cold water
½ c water

1 T cornstarch
6 T sugar

Dissolve 1 T cornstarch in 1 T cold water. Add ½ c water. Cook until thick and clear, cool thoroughly. Beat 3 egg whites until foamy, add 6 T sugar and beat until stiff. Add cooled mixture to egg whites. Spread on pie. Bake at 350 degrees until browned about 12-15 minutes.

Shaker Lemon Pie

2 large lemons
2 c sugar

4 eggs, well beaten
2 9-inch unbaked pie shells

Slice unpeeled lemons paper-thin. Remove seeds, add sugar and mix well.
Let stand 2 hours or longer, stirring occasionally. Thoroughly blend eggs
into the lemon mixture. Turn into an unbaked pie shell, arranging lemon
slices evenly. Slice the remaining pie shell to make a vented top. Bake at
450 degrees for 15 minutes; reduce the heat to 375 degrees and cook for 20
minutes until "a silver knife inserted near the edge comes out clean."

*Martha Stewart enjoyed this recipe on a visit to Shakertown near
Harrodsburg, Kentucky, and took two pies home with her.*

Key Lime Pie ... very good and very easy

1 pie shell, baked and cooled

Filling:
1 can sweetened condensed milk
1 T grated key lime rind
½ c lime juice
¼ t salt
2 slightly beaten egg yolks

Meringue:
3 egg whites
3 T sugar
Beat until foamy then gradually
mix in sugar and beat until stiff
peaks form.

Stir all filling ingredients until thickened (a result of a reaction to the milk
and lime juice). (Optional: 2-3 drops green cake coloring) Pour into crust,
and cover with meringue. Bake for 10-15 minutes at 350 degrees until
lightly browned.

Some people make the world more special just by being in it.
— Unknown

Lucky-To-Have-Any-Left Pie

First layer:

2 c flour
2 stick butter
1 c pecans

Mix and press into 13 x 9 inch Pyrex pan. Bake for 20 minutes in a 325-degree oven. Cool.

Second layer:

1 8-oz cream cheese
1 c powdered sugar
1 9-oz Kool Whip

Mix with mixer and spread over crust.

Third layer:

2 small pkgs butter-pecan instant pudding mix
3½ c milk

Mix well and pour over 2nd layer

Fourth layer:

9 oz Kool Whip
¾ c chopped pecans

Put on top of 3rd layer and sprinkle with chopped pecans

Decadent Triple-Layer Mud Pie

3 squares semi-sweet baking chocolate or ½ c chocolate chips, melted
¼ c can sweetened condensed milk
1 Oreo pie crust

½ c chopped pecans
2 c cold milk
2 pkg small instant chocolate pudding
8 oz Kool whip, thawed

Mix chocolate and condensed milk until well blended. Pour into crust, sprinkle with pecans. Pour milk into large bowl. Add pudding mixes. Beat with wire whisk 2 minutes or until well blended. (Mixture will be thick) Spoon 1½ cups of the pudding over pecans in crust. Add ½ of the whipped topping to remaining pudding. Stir with wire whisk until blended. Spread over pudding in crust; top with remaining whipped topping. Refrigerate 3 hours. Makes 10 serving.

"When women are depressed, they either eat or go shopping. Men invade another country. It's a whole different way of thinking."
— Elaine Boosler

Minty Grasshopper Pie

1 ready-crust chocolate pie crust
8 oz cream cheese, softened
1 sweetened condensed milk
8 oz Kool Whip, thawed

16 Keebler Fudgeshoppe
Grasshopper cookies, coarsely
    crushed
green food coloring

With mixer, beat cream cheese until fluffy; gradually beat in sweetened condensed milk until smooth. Stir in a few drops of food coloring. Add crushed cookies, fold in Kool whip, and pour into pie crust. Chill at least 3 hours. Served chilled. Refrigerate leftovers.

Chocolate Chess Pie

1¼ c sugar
¼ c margarine
10 T evaporated milk
¼ c cocoa

2 eggs
1½ t vanilla
1 unbaked pie crust

Mix sugar, cocoa and melted margarine in medium bowl. Add eggs; beat well. Blend in milk and vanilla. Bake in pie shell at 350 degrees until tester comes out clear, 35-40 minutes.

Ozark Pudding

1 egg
2 heaping T flour
⅛ t salt
½ chopped nuts

¾ cup sugar
¼ t baking powder
½ c chopped apples
1 t vanilla

Beat egg, and sugar until light and fluffy. Sift together flour, baking powder, salt and mix with egg mixture. Fold in apples and nuts. Add vanilla. Bake 30 minutes at 325 degrees in a buttered Pyrex dish. Serve with hard sauce.

Hard Sauce for Ozark Pudding:

1 c light brown sugar
½ c butter

1 t bourbon whiskey

Sift sugar and beat it into butter. Add bourbon and warm.

All I really need is love, but a little chocolate now and then, doesn't hurt!
— Lucy Van Pelt (in *Peanuts*, by Charles M. Schulz)

Nestle's Grand Prize Winner Pie

9-inch deep-dish pie shell, baked
⅓ c chocolate chips
1 T butter
20 vanilla caramels
⅓ c heavy whipping cream
1½ c salted peanuts, coarsely chopped
½ c milk
1⅓ c chocolate chips
15 large marshmallows
¼ t vanilla
2 c Kool Whip

Topping:
3 vanilla caramels
2 T heavy whipping cream
1 T butter
whipped cream
⅓ c chocolate chips

In a small heavy saucepan, combine the ⅓ cup chocolate chips and 1 T butter. Cook and stir over low heat until melted and smooth. Spread chocolate around bottom and sides of the baked pie shell; refrigerate 15 minutes or until chocolate is set.

In another small saucepan, combine 20 caramels and the ⅓ c heavy whipping cream. Cook and stir over medium heat until the caramels are melted and mixture is smooth. Stir in the peanuts. Spoon peanut mixture into pie shell; cover and refrigerator while preparing chocolate mixture.

For chocolate mixture; in a medium saucepan combine milk, 1⅓ cups chocolate chips and the marshmallows. Cook and stir over low heat until chocolate and marshmallows are melted and mixture is smooth. Remove from heat; stir in vanilla; set aside until cool.

When chocolate mixture is cool, add the Kool whip. Spoon the chocolate mixture over the peanut layer in pie shell. Refrigerate until set, at least 3 hours. Before serving, in a small saucepan, melt 3 caramels, 2 tablespoons of heavy cream and I tablespoon of butter over low heat. Let cool slightly. Top each serving with caramel mixture, Kool Whip, and remaining chocolate chips. Makes 10-12 servings.

Oreo Dessert

1 bag of Oreo cookies, crushed
8 oz cream cheese
7 T butter, melted
1 box powdered sugar
2 small instant vanilla pudding
3 c milk
8 oz Kool Whip

Crush cookies. Mix cream cheese, butter and powdered sugar together. Mix pudding and milk together, then add Kool Whip. Layer cookies, cream cheese mixture, and pudding mixture and refrigerate.

October Pie

Crust:
1 pg yellow cake mix, divided;
1 egg
½ c melted margarine
Filling:
2 eggs
⅔ c milk
1 can Libby's pumpkin pie mix

Topping:
1 c reserved cake mix
1 tsp cinnamon
¼ c sugar
2 T melted butter

Crust: Remove 1 cup cake mix and save. To remainder of mix add margarine and beaten egg. Mix and spread on bottom of greased 9 x 13 inch pan.

Filling: Combine pie mix with 2 beaten eggs and milk; Spread over crust.

Topping: Combine and mix with fork and sprinkle over filling. Bake 45 to 50 minutes at 350 degrees. Refrigerate to store.

Ozark Pie

¾ c sugar
¾ c flour
1 egg
1¼ t baking powder

⅛ t salt
1 c apples, cut up
1 c pecans, chopped
1 t vanilla

Beat egg. Add sugar. Add sifted flour, salt, baking powder. Add nuts, apples, and vanilla. Spread and bake in a buttered 8-inch pie pan at 350 degrees for 35 minutes. Serve with whipped cream or ice cream.

Peach Delight

32 oz peaches, with juice
½ c pecans

Butter Pecan cake mix
6 oz melted butter

Pour peaches into 9 x 11 inch Pyrex baking dish. Sprinkle dry cake mix on top. Sprinkle pecans over the cake mix and pour melted butter on top. Bake for 1 hour at 350 degrees.

"Vegetables are a must on a diet. I suggest carrot cake, zucchini bread, and pumpkin pie."
— Jim Davis, "Garfield"

Peach Crisp

Pie Filling:

1 29-oz can sliced peaches	1 c packed brown sugar
2 T cornstarch	1 T honey
¼ t cinnamon	¼ t nutmeg
½ c lemon juice	½ c raisins
½ c chopped pecans	

Topping:

1 c flour	½ c melted butter
½ c sugar	optional: vanilla ice cream

Pie Filling:
Drain peaches, reserving syrup in saucepan. Set peaches aside. Stir brown sugar, cornstarch, honey, cinnamon, nutmeg and syrup until smooth. Bring to boil and stir for 2 minutes until thick. Add lemon juice, pecans, and peaches. Pour into greased 2-qt dish.

Topping:
Combine flour, sugar and butter. Sprinkle over peach mixture. Bake 350 degrees for 35 minutes. Serve with ice cream if desired.

Peach Cobbler

1 c flour	½ c milk
1 c sugar	1 stick margarine
1 t baking powder	4 c sliced peaches

Melt margarine in 9 x 13 inch pan. Mix flour, sugar, baking powder and a dash of salt. Add milk slowly. Peel and slice peaches and add about ½ cup water and ½ cup sugar and simmer over low heat. Let sugar dissolve and peaches get hot. Pour batter over melted butter —do not stir. Bake in oven for about 7-10 minutes, letting batter rise some; add peaches and syrup. Do not stir. Bake at 350 degrees for 45 minutes or until cake on top is done. Serve warm with ice cream and enjoy.

Peanut Butter Chiffon Pie

1 envelope unflavored gelatin
½ c boiling water
8 oz cream cheese
1 c powdered sugar

½ c favorite peanut butter
8 oz Kool Whip
1 9-in graham cracker crust
¼ c finely chopped peanuts, optional

Dissolve gelatin in boiling water. Cool to lukewarm. Whip cheese until soft and fluffy. Beat in sugar and peanut butter. Slowly add gelatin mixture, blending thoroughly. Fold Kool Whip into mixture. Chill until firm, 1-2 hours. *Optiona*l: Drizzle with Hershey's chocolate syrup before serving.

Peanut Butter Pie

10 inch pie shell, baked and cooled
1 c chunky peanut butter
2 c sugar
2 8-oz cream cheese, softened
1 T butter, softened
2 t vanilla
1½ c Kool Whip

Sauce:
1 c chocolate chips
¼ c coffee liquor

In a large bowl combine peanut butter, sugar, cream cheese, butter and vanilla. Mix well. Fold in the Kool Whip. Spoon into the prepared pie shell. Refrigerate at least 6 hours. Before serving melt together the chocolate chips and coffee liquor and drizzle over the pie.

Two Pecan Pies

2 unbaked pie shells
½ c margarine, melted
5 eggs, well beaten
1 c coconut

2 c sugar
1½ c dark corn syrup
1 T lemon juice
¾ c pecans

Mix all ingredients and place in 2 pie shells. Bake at 425 degrees for 10 minutes, reduce heat to 300 degrees and bake for 50 min. Will freeze.

Pineapple Meringue … a special family favorite

8 egg whites
½ t salt
2 t vanilla
1 T vinegar

2 c sugar
1 large can of crushed pineapple,
   partially drained
8 oz Kool Whip

Preheat oven to 450 degrees. Beat egg whites, salt, vanilla and vinegar on high speed until soft peaks appear. Gradually add sugar, small amount at a time until stiff peaks appear. Divide into two 9-inch cake pans lined with brown paper bags cut to fit. Grease only on side next to pan. Turn oven down to 300 degrees and bake for one hour. Cool on wire racks. Can store in pans for several days before using.

Run a knife around edge of pan to remove meringue, and peel off paper. Place on serving dish with a lip. Partially drain the pineapple and spread half on top of first layer. Top with ⅓ of the Kool Whip. Add second layer and top with remaining pineapple and cream.

Variation:
Add red food coloring to the meringue and use fresh strawberries, cut and sugared, instead of crushed pineapple.

"I sometimes use 1 cup of fresh strawberries, cut and sugared, in addition to crushed pineapple, and strawberry-flavored Kool Whip instead of plain Kool Whip. Yumm"

Pineapple Coconut Pie

1½ cups sugar
1 c crushed pineapple
   (do not drain)
3 lightly beaten eggs

3 T flour
1 c flaked coconut
¾ stick margarine
1 unbaked pie shell

Preheat oven to 350 degrees. Stir together sugar, pineapple, eggs, flour and coconut in a bowl. Melt butter and add to other ingredients. Pour filling into pie shell. Bake 1 hour or until filling is set and brown.

They are not gone who live on in the hearts they left behind.
— Native American Proverb

Pineapple Pie … easy and good

1 large can crushed pineapple   1 graham cracker crust
5 oz instant vanilla pudding   Kool Whip
1 c sour cream

Mix dry pudding mix with sour cream and pineapple juice. Add
pineapple and mix and pour into crust. Ice with Kool whip. Refrigerate.

Dickinson Pumpkin Pie

1 c cooked pumpkin   ½ to 1 t allspice
1 egg   ¼ t nutmeg
1 T cream or milk   ¼ ginger
1 c sugar   1 T melted butter
¼ t cinnamon   1 unbaked pie shell

Beat egg, add sugar, spices, cream, pumpkin and melted butter. Blend.
Pour into unbaked crust; bake 10 minutes at 450 degrees, then 30 minutes
at 350 degrees. Serve with whipped cream.

*This recipe has been handed down in my family for seven generations. It
is THE Dickinson Pumpkin Pie recipe that my Aunt 'Nez Dickinson sent
to* The Louisville Courier Journal's *Cissy Greg, in contradiction to an
editorial that stated "the best place for pumpkins was to leave them in the
field." Aunt 'Nez wrote "I didn't like pumpkin pie either, until I married
and moved to Kentucky from Louisiana." "Then," she said, "I ate a
piece of pumpkin pie made by my husband's mother, from a recipe
handed down from her grandmother (ca.1880) and I changed my mind!"*

*Aunt 'Nez recommended that the pie was never to be eaten stone cold, but
I have known Dickinsons to eat it in any form, at any time, even for
breakfast. My mother would reduce the sugar to ¾ c per pie and triple
this recipe to make two pies."*

Pumpkin Pecan Pie

4 slightly beaten eggs
2 c canned or mashed
   cooked pumpkin
1 c sugar
½ c dark corn syrup

1 t vanilla
½ t cinnamon
¼ t salt
1 unbaked 9-inch pie shell
1 c chopped pecans

Combine ingredients except pecans. Pour into pie shell and top with pecans. Bake at 350 degrees for 40 minutes or until set.

Pie Crust

2 c flour*
11 T shortening

5-6 T ice water
1 t salt

Sift flour into a mixing bowl. Add shortening and cut with pastry blender or 2 forks. Mix ice water and salt together and add to flour mixture by tossing with fingertips. Roll out on wax paper into a 10-inch circle and place in pie dish. Turn under edges and pinch with fingers or a fork. Cook for 12-15 minutes in a 450-degree oven.

Add ½ teaspoon baking powder for each cup of flour, for a much lighter pie shell.

Glazed Raspberry Pie

1 pie shell, baked
5 c fresh raspberries, divided
1 c water, divided
1 c sugar
3 T cornstarch

2 T lemon juice
3 oz cream cheese, softened
1 T butter or margarine, softened
1 T milk
Kool Whip

Bake pie shell. Cool. In a saucepan, combine ⅔ cup raspberries and ⅔ cup water. Simmer uncovered, for 3 minutes. Strain raspberries and discard seeds; set juice aside. In another saucepan, combine sugar, cornstarch and remaining water until smooth. Add raspberry juice. Bring to a boil over medium heat; cook and stir for 2 minutes or until thickened. Remove for the heat; add lemon juice. Cool. In a small mixing bowl, beat cream cheese, butter and milk until smooth. Spread on the bottom and up the sides of the baked pie shell. Fill pastry shell with the remaining raspberries. Slowly pour glaze over berries. Refrigerate until serving. Garnish with Kool Whip. Serves 8.

Rhubarb Pie

2 c rhubarb, cut in ½ inch pieces　　2 T butter or margarine
1 c sugar　　2 unbaked pie shells
3 T flour

Mix rhubarb, sugar and flour together and place in unbaked pie shell. Cut butter up over the mixture. Add top crust. Seal and puncture this crust with a fork. Sprinkle with sugar and bake for 45 minutes in a 350 degree oven.

Rum Pies ... terrific, timeless desserts

2 deep-dish graham cracker pie　　½ c water
　　crusts　　1 pint of whipping cream
6 egg yolks　　½ c good rum
1 c sugar　　chocolate to grate on top
1 envelope gelatin

Beat egg yolks and sugar until light. Dissolve gelatin in water and bring to a boil. Pour gelatin into egg mixture, beating briskly Cool. Beat the whipping cream until stiff. Fold cream into egg mixture. Add the rum. Pour into two graham cracker crusts and put into refrigerator. Grate a little chocolate on top.

Tanya's Iron Skillet Chocolate Pie...super

1 baked pie shell　　1 rounded T butter
1 c sugar　　2 eggs, separated
2 rounded T flour　　1 c milk
3 rounded T cocoa　　1 t vanilla
　　Kool Whip

Mix sugar, flour and cocoa in a bowl. Melt butter in iron skillet, add sugar mixture and mix lightly. Combine beaten egg yolks and milk, add to mixture a little at a time, stirring constantly. Cook slowly until thick; add vanilla and blend well. Pour into baked pie shell. Serve with Kool Whip

Tanya always doubles this recipe for one pie. My son likes this pie much better than his own mother's chocolate pie!

Strawberry Delight

2 c frozen whole strawberries,
   thawed
1 pkg (3.4 oz) instant vanilla
   pudding mix

12 oz frozen Kool Whip, thawed
1 graham cracker crust
½ c flaked coconut, toasted

In a mixing bowl, crush strawberries. Add food coloring if desired. Beat in pudding mix until smooth. Fold in whipped topping. Pour into crust; sprinkle with coconut. Chill until serving. Store leftovers in the refrigerator. Serves. 6-8.

To Toast Coconut: Spread the flaked coconut on a baking sheet and bake at 350 degrees until light brown, stirring often, generally 6-10 minutes.

Strawberry Tarts . . . quick and very good

6 Graham Cracker tart shells
1 c strawberry gel (found in
   produce department)
1½ c sliced strawberries

4 oz cream cheese, softened
½ c sugar
1 T sour cream
1 t vanilla

Slice strawberries and mix with gel. Combine cream cheese, sugar, sour cream, and vanilla and place a heaping tablespoon is each shell. Spoon strawberries and gel on top in each tart.

Millionaire Pie

I can Eagle Brand condensed
   milk (can use fat free)
9 oz Kool Whip
4 T lemon juice

1 lrg can crushed pineapple,
   drained well
½ c chopped pecans
2 graham cracker crusts

Combine condensed milk and lemon juice; mix well. Fold in Kool Whip; stir in well-drained pineapple and pecans. Spread into 2 prepared crusts and chill.

Not to know what happened before you were born
is to always remain a child.
— Cicero

Peanut Butter Chocolate Dessert

25 Oreo cookies, divided
2 T margarine, melted
8 oz cream cheese, softened
½ c peanut butter

1½ cups powdered sugar, divided
16 oz Kool Whip, thawed and divided
15 miniature peanut butter cups, chopped
1 c cold milk
1 small instant chocolate pudding mix

Crush Oreos and toss with the butter. Press into the bottom of an un-greased 9-inch square dish. Save about ¼ of the crushed Oreos for topping. In a mixing bowl, beat the cream cheese, peanut butter and 1 cup of the powdered sugar until smooth. Fold in half of the Kool Whip. Spread over crust carefully. Sprinkle with peanut butter cups.

Beat the milk; pudding mix and remaining powdered sugar on low speed for 2 minutes. Fold in remaining whipped topping. Spread over peanut butter cups. Sprinkle with remaining Oreo crumbs. Cover and chill for at least 3 hours. Yield: 12-16 servings

Transparent Pie … an old Southern favorite

3 eggs
¾ c light corn syrup
⅔ c sugar
⅓ c butter, melted

¼ c molasses
1 t vanilla
1½ c chopped walnuts
9 inch unbaked pie shell

In a bowl, whisk eggs, corn syrup, sugar, butter, molasses and vanilla until blended; stir in walnuts. Pour into pastry shell. Cover edges with foil. Bake at 350 degrees for 25 minutes, remove foil. Bake 12-17 minutes longer or until top of the pie is set and crust is golden brown. Cool on wire rack. Refrigerate for several hours before cutting, if possible. Serves 8.

To prevent a bottom piecrust from becoming soggy, grease pie pans with margarine. The crust will be soft and flaky.

Southern Stack Pie ... unique, and very, very rich

4 pie crusts, unbaked
6 eggs, beaten
1 c Carnation evaporated milk
3 c sugar
¾ c margarine
1 t vanilla

Caramel topping:
2 c brown sugar
1 c margarine
½ c whole milk
1 t vanilla
powdered sugar

Combine eggs, milk, sugar and margarine. Microwave 3 minutes. Stir. Microwave 2 minutes. Stir in vanilla. Heat oven to 350 degrees.

Choose one pie crust to use as the bottom, and leave as is. Carefully trim back the edges of the other 3 crusts, so the crusts cover the bottom of the pan and up the sides, but there is no overhang onto the lip of the pie pan. Fill each pie crust with equal amounts of filling. Bake the pies 30 minutes. Cool.

To make the topping: Bring brown sugar, margarine and milk just to a boil, stirring. Remove from the heat, stir in the vanilla. Beat in enough powdered sugar to make an icing. Spread part if the icing over the filling in the bottom pie crust, kept in the pan.

Carefully remove one of the other trimmed crusts from its pan, and place on top of the first, and top with icing. Then stack the third and the fourth crust the same way, topping each with caramel icing. Slice into wedges to serve. Serves 12. 850 calories

Sara's Strawberry Pie

1 pkg vanilla pudding
1 pkg strawberry jello
1 cooked pie shell

1 pkg Cool Whip
1 pkg fresh strawberries

Cook vanilla pudding with 2 cups water and bring to a boil. When boiling and thick, remove from heat and add box of strawberry jello. Stir until dissolved. It will make a clear, red glaze.

Cut strawberries and place in pie shell. When glaze is cool, pour over berries and cover with Cool Whip. Top with a strawberry!

Can use sugar free puddings and lite Cool Whip for sugar free dessert. Very good!

Heavenly Delight

Vanilla wafers
2 eggs
1 stick butter
1 box powdered sugar

½ pint whipping cream
1 small can crushed pineapple
pecans, chopped (about 1 cup)

Line bottom of 6 x 10 dish with wafer crumbs. Melt butter and mix with eggs and powdered sugar. Pour mixture over crumbs. Beat cream into peaks and add drained pineapple. Spread over egg and sugar mixture and sprinkle with about 1-cup wafer crumbs. Sprinkle chopped pecans on top. Cover and refrigerate.

The Dutch are the biggest eaters of candy, at 65 pounds per person each year; Americans eat about 21 pounds per year.

Cakes

Linda's Chocolate Flavored Angel Food Cake

1 Angel food cake mix   ½ t cinnamon
3 T cocoa

Make cake according to directions on box, adding cocoa and cinnamon.
Bake in an prepared Angel food cake pan following box directions. Cool
upside down on a pop bottle. When thoroughly cooled, run a knife
around the outside of the cake to loosen. Turn upside down on a serving
platter and remove outside of pan. Run knife under bottom of pan and lift
off.

Apple Dopple Cake

1½ c oil   1 t salt
2 c sugar   1 t soda
3 eggs   3 c fine chopped apples
3 c flour   1½ c nuts
2 t vanilla   6-oz pkg. butterscotch chips

Preheat oven to 350 degrees. Cream oil, sugar and eggs until smooth.
Measure flour, salt and soda together. Beat in oil mixture. Beat in
vanilla. Fold in apples, nuts and chips. Pour into a well-greased and
floured bundt pan; bake until a toothpick comes out clean, about 1 hour
and 20 minutes.

Apple Pie Cake

⅔ c self-rising flour   1 t vanilla
1¾ c sugar   ¾ c oil
1 t cloves   3 eggs
1 t nutmeg   1 can apple pie filling
1 heaping t cinnamon   1 c pecans, chopped

Mix the dry ingredients together; add all other ingredients. Mix well. Pour
into greased and floured tube pan. Bake for 1 to 1¼ hours at 350 degrees.
Cool in pan for 10 minutes before taking out.

Glaze for Cake
½-¾ box powdered sugar   ¼ t vanilla
½ stick margarine   1 T milk
½ t cinnamon
Mix this to soft spreading consistency, and smooth over top of the cake.

Apple Spice Snack Cake ... simple and delicious

1 pkg spice cake mix   2 eggs
21 oz apple pie filling   2 T oil

In a mixing bowl, combine all ingredients. Beat on medium speed for 2 minutes. Pour into a greased 13 x 9 x 2 inch baking pan. Bake at 350 degrees for 30-35 minutes or until a toothpick inserted near the center comes out clean. Cool on wire rack. Makes 15 servings.

Apple Pudding

2 cups flour	¼ cup butter
2 t cinnamon	2 eggs
1 t salt	1 cup nuts (walnuts or pecans)
1 t baking soda	4 cups Granny Smith Apples
2 cups sugar	

Mix dry ingredients together. Add remaining ingredients. Bake 40 minutes in an 11x13 inch dish in a 350-degree oven. Serve with the sauce below and Kool Whip.

Sauce:

1 cup butter	1 cup Half and Half
2 t vanilla	pinch of nutmeg
2 cups sugar	

Mix ingredients and cook 5 minutes in a double boiler. Do not boil.

Better-Than-Sex Cake

1 box strawberry cake mix   8-oz Kool Whip
1 pkg frozen strawberries (thawed)   chopped pecans
1 large box instant vanilla pudding

Make cake according to directions on box and bake in a greased 11 x 13 inch pan. Use a fork to punch holes in cake then pour strawberries with juice over cake. Mix vanilla pudding according to package directions. Pour over cake. Top with Kool Whip and nuts. Chill.

Banana Cake

2 medium ripe bananas, mashed
1 c flour
¾ c chopped walnuts
⅔ c sugar
1 c cornstarch
1 egg, slightly beaten
1 T orange juice
1 t baking soda

1 t vanilla
1 t salt

Frosting:
½ c soft butter
1½ c powdered sugar
1 T orange juice
1 T grated orange peel

Preheat oven to 350 degrees. Mix dry ingredients. Stir in remaining ingredients. Pour into greased and floured 8 x 8 inch baking dish. Bake for 30 minutes or until toothpick comes out clean when poked into cakes' center. Set aside to cool before icing.

For icing, combine all the ingredients, mix until fluffy, and spread on cake.

Sour Cream Apple Cake

½ c finely chopped walnuts
1 t cinnamon
1½ c sugar, separated
½ c margarine
2 c flour

1 c sour cream
3 eggs
1 t baking soda
1 t baking powdered
1 t vanilla
1-2 apples, peeled and cored

Mix and set aside the walnuts, cinnamon and ½ cup sugar. In a small bowl, beat margarine with 1 cup of sugar until light and fluffy. Add flour and remaining ingredients, except apples, and beat on low speed until blended. Increase speed to medium, beat three more minutes

Spread half of batter into a greased and floured bundt pan, sprinkle with one half of the sugar-walnut mixture. Lay slices of apples on top of sugar mixture. Pour rest of batter on top. Bake 45 to 60 minutes at 350 degrees. Cool for 10 minutes in pan and remove.

No one can make you feel inferior without your consent."
— Eleanor Roosevelt

Black Forest Cake

1 German chocolate or devil's
    food cake mix
eggs and shortening as called
    for on the box
⅓ c plus 4 T rum

1 c mini chocolate chips
1 can cherry pie filling
16 oz Kool Whip
shaved chocolate and cocktail
    cherries for garnish

Prepare cake according to directions on box except substitute ⅓ cup rum for ⅓ cup of the water. When mix is prepared, stir in mini morsels. Bake in two 9-inch pans. Stir 4T rum into cherry pie filling. Allow cake to cool. Place first layer on a platter, spread ½ pie filling and ½ Kool Whip. Add next layer and repeat pie filling and Kool Whip

Blackberry Cake ... a family favorite

2 c sugar
1 c shortening
1-2 c blackberries canned or
    fresh with ¼ c water
1 c buttermilk
1 T soda

3 eggs
3 c flour
dash of salt
1 t of cloves, nutmeg, cinnamon,
    and allspice
½ c chopped nuts

Mix all ingredients well and bake in a large sheet cake pan at 350 degrees for 35-40 minutes or until toothpick in center is clean. Frost with Cream Cheese Recipe below or a Caramel Icing.

Cream Cheese Icing:
8-oz pkg cream cheese
1 box powdered cheese

½ c margarine
1 t vanilla

Mix all ingredients, beat well and spread on cake.

Boston Cream Pie, or Boston Cream Cake?

Yellow cake mix

Filling:
2 small pkgs instant vanilla
    pudding
1 cup Kool Whip
2 cups milk

Frosting:
½ c sour cream
2 cups powdered sugar
1 cups chocolate chips
1 t vanilla

Prepare cake according to directions. And bake in two 9-10 inch greased pans lined with wax paper. Cool in pans 10 minutes.

For filling, combine pudding and milk. Whisk until smooth and slightly thickened. Whisk in Kool Whip and spread in center of cake. Add second layer. For frosting, whisk sour cream and margarine until well blended. Whisk in powdered sugar and mix until blended. Melt chocolate chips in microwave and stir into sugar mixture. Stir in vanilla and enough milk to reach desired spreading consistency. Spread over top layer. Refrigerate.

Bread Pudding

1-lb loaf French style bread (the
    firmer the better)
3 eggs
3¼ c milk
¾ c sugar

2 t vanilla
¼ c raisins
¼ c pecans
¼ t cinnamon

Break bread in small pieces and put in large bowl. Add sugar and cinnamon. Combine milk, beaten eggs and vanilla. Add to bread mix, and allow to soak for 5 minutes. Place ½ mix in a 2 quart casserole dish. Layer pecans and raisins. Top with rest of mix. Bake at 350 degrees for 30 minutes or until lightly browned. Serve warm with bourbon sauce.

Bourbon Sauce

1 stick butter
1 c sugar
½ t baking soda
1 T corn syrup

2 T bourbon
½ c buttermilk
1 t vanilla

In a saucepan mix all ingredients. Bring to a boil for 1 minute. Serve warm over bread pudding.

Cinnamon Sauce ... for bread pudding & dumplings

⅓ c sugar   ¼ t cinnamon
2 t cornstarch   ⅔ c water
dash salt

Mix dry ingredients, then stir in water and heat over medium heat. Bring to boil, stirring frequently. Serve warm over bread pudding, or dumplings. Add raisins if you like. Makes ⅔ cup.

I usually double this for the family. Pepperidge Farm makes Frozen Apple Dumplings that make a good and quick dessert with this sauce.

Brownie Torte Cake

1 pkg brownie mix (for a 13 x 9   ½ c packed brown sugar
   inch pan)   1 ½ t maple flavoring
½ c chopped walnuts   1 t vanilla extract
2 c whipping cream   chocolate curls and additional
2 t instant coffee   walnuts, optional

Prepare batter for brownie mix according to package directions for cake-like brownies. Stir in walnuts. Pour into two greased 9-in round baking pans. Bake at 350 degrees for 20-22 minutes or until a toothpick comes out clean. Cool for 10 minutes before removing from pans to wire racks to cool completely.

In a bowl, beat cream and coffee granules until stiff peaks form. Gradually beat in brown sugar, maple flavoring and vanilla. Spread 1 ½ cups over one brownie layer; top with second layer. Spread remaining cream mixture over top and sides of torte. Garnish with chocolate curls or walnuts if desired. Store in the refrigerator. Serves 12.

Cherries Jubilee

2 sticks butter
2 c flour
1 c pecans, chopped fine
8 oz cream cheese

1 lb confectioners sugar
4 c Kool Whip
1 can cherry pie filling

Mix first 3 ingredients. Pat into 9 x 13 inch pan. Bake at 400 degrees for 20 minutes. Mix cheese and sugar, fold Kool Whip into cheese mixture. Spread over cooled crust. Cool in refrigerator. Add 1 can cherry pie filling on top.

Chocolate Cherry Upside-Down Cake ... quick

1 box Chocolate cake mix
21-oz can cherry pie filling

Spread the cherry pie filling evenly over the bottom of a greased 13 x 9 baking pan. Mix the cake mix according to the directions on the box. Pour batter evenly over cherry pie filling. Bake in 350 degree oven for 30-35 minutes or till cake tests done. Cool 10 minutes in pan; invert and cool. Serve with Kool Whip.

Easy Cherry Dessert

2 c crushed graham cracker crumbs
½ c melted margarine
¾ c sugar, divided

8 oz cream cheese, softened
2 eggs
1 can cherry pie filling
Kool Whip

Combine crumbs, margarine, and ¼ cup sugar together. Press into pie shell. In another bowl beat together cream cheese, ½ cup sugar and eggs. Pour over crust and bake at 350 degrees for 35 minutes. Chill. Top with cherry pie filling. Top with Kool Whip when served.

Carrot Cake ... a grand prize winner

Cake:
1¼ c oil
2 c sugar
2 c flour
2 t cinnamon
2 t baking powder
1 t baking soda
1 t salt
4 eggs
4 c finely shredded carrots
1 c raisins
1 c chopped pecans

Filling:
1 c sugar
2 T flour
¼ t salt
1 c whipping cream
½ c butter or margarine
1 c chopped pecans
1 t vanilla

Frosting:
¾ c butter or margarine, softened
2 3-oz pkgs cream cheese,
     softened
1 t vanilla
3 c powdered sugar

For the filling: Combine sugar, flour and salt in a heavy saucepan. Stir in cream; add butter. Cook and stir over medium heat until the butter is melted; bring to a boil. Reduce heat. Simmer, uncovered, for 30 minutes, stirring occasionally. Stir in nuts and vanilla. Set aside to cool.

In a mixing bowl, beat oil and sugar for 1 minute. Combine flour, cinnamon, baking powder, baking soda and salt; add to the creamed mixture alternately with eggs. Mix well. Stir in carrots, raisins and nuts. Pour into three greased and floured 9 in round baking pans. Bake at 350 degrees for 35-40 minutes or until a wooden pick inserted near the center comes out clean. Cool in pans 10 minutes; remove to wire racks and cool completely.

For frosting, beat butter, cream cheese and vanilla until smooth. Gradually beat in sugar. Spread filling between cake layers. Frost sides and top of cake. Store in the refrigerator. Serves 16-20.

Chocolate-Amaretto Cheesecake... fantastic & easy

10 chocolate wafers, finely crushed
1½ cups light cream cheese
1 c sugar
1 c 1% low-fat cottage cheese
¼ c plus 2 T cocoa
¼ c flour
¼ c amaretto*

1 t vanilla extract
¼ t salt
1 egg
2 T chocolate chips

Topping:
1 c chocolate chips
½ c sour cream

Sprinkle chocolate wafer crumbs in bottom of a 9-inch spring form pan. Set aside. Blend cream cheese, and next 7 ingredients, in a food processor until smooth. Add egg and process until blended. Fold in chocolate chips. Slowly pour mixture over crumbs in pan. Bake at 300 degrees for 65-70 minutes or until cheesecake is set. Let cool in pan on wire rack. Cover and chill at least 8 hours. Remove sides from pan and transfer to a serving platter.

Add topping made from 1 cup melted chocolate chips and ½ cup sour cream.

Amaretto is an Italian liqueur flavored with almond, found in the baking section at the grocery store.

Easy Banana Cake

1 yellow cake mix
Icing:
½ stick butter

½ c brown sugar, packed
1-2 bananas
2½ c powdered sugar

Mix cake according to box directions. Bake in 2 (9 inch) round cake pans. Cool.

Icing
Melt butter and brown sugar in pan. Mash bananas, and add to butter/sugar mixture. Stir. Cool. Add powdered sugar and beat until ready to spread. Spread between layers and sides of cake.

Lelia's Chocolate Cheese Cake

Crust:
1½ c crushed Oreo cookies
¼ c margarine (melted)

Gouache Topping:
2 c whipping cream
8 oz chocolate chips

Filling:
3 8-oz pkg cream cheese, softened
1¼ c sugar
6 eggs
1 pt sour cream
⅓ c flour
2 t vanilla
8 oz chocolate chips, melted

Crust:
Preheat oven to 350 degrees. Generously grease a 9 x 13 spring form pan with butter. Mix crust ingredients in bowl until well blended. Press mixture into bottom and sides of pan. Cook for 10 minutes.

Filling:
With electric mixer on low speed or with a wooden spoon, beat cream cheese in a large bowl until soft. Gradually beat in sugar until light and fluffy. Beat in eggs, one at a time until well blended. Stir in sour cream, flour vanilla until smooth. Cool in refrigerator.

Gouache Topping:
The next day, warm cream to just beginning to boil, and take off the stove. Add chips and stir until dissolved. Spread over top of cake. Chill in refrigerator.

Lemon Cheesecake ... in three easy steps

2 8-oz pkg cream cheese
½ c sugar
1 T fresh lemon juice
½ t grated lemon peel
½ t vanilla
2 eggs
graham cracker crust

Mix cream cheese, sugar, juice, peel and vanilla on medium speed until well blended. Add eggs; mix thoroughly. Pour into crust. Bake at 350 degrees for 30 minutes or until center is almost set. Cool. Refrigerate 3 hours or overnight.

Chocolate Chip Cheesecake ... easy

1 Graham Cracker crust
2 3-oz pkg cream cheese,
   softened
14 oz can sweetened condensed
   milk
1 egg
1 t vanilla

1 c mini-chocolate chips
1 t flour

Glaze:
½ c mini chocolate chips
¼ c whipping cream

Preheat oven to 350 degrees. With a mixer, beat cheese until fluffy, gradually beat in sweetened condensed milk until smooth. Add egg, vanilla; mix well. Toss chips with flour; stir into cheese mixture. Pour into pie crust. Bake 35 minutes or until center springs back when lightly touched. Cool and top with glaze. Serve chilled. Refrigerate leftovers.

To make glaze, in a small saucepan, over low heat, melt chocolate chips with whipping cream. Cook and stir until thickened and smooth. Immediately spread over pie.

Crust-less Microwave Cheesecake Pie

2 8-oz pkg cream cheese, softened
⅔ c plus 3 T sugar, divided
3 eggs
1½ t vanilla, divided

¾ t fresh lemon juice, divided
16 oz sour cream
1 can cherry pie filling

Coat a microwave-safe 9-inch-deep pie plate with nonstick cooking spray. In a large bowl, with an electric beater on medium speed, beat the cream cheese and ⅔ cup sugar until smooth. Beat in the eggs, one at a time, then beat in ½ t vanilla and ¼ t lemon juice; pour into the pie plate.

Meanwhile, in a medium bowl, combine the sour cream and the remaining 3 T sugar, 1 t vanilla and ½ t lemon juice; mix well, then pour over the top of the pie.

Microwave at 70% power for 3 minutes. Let cool, then cover and chill for at least four hours before serving. Add can of cherry pie filling and serve.

Chocolate Ice Box Dessert

2 small pkg chocolate chips   1 c chopped nuts
2 T sugar   1 pint whipping cream
3 eggs, separated and beaten   1 large angel food cake

Melt chocolate chips and sugar in a double boiler and remove from heat.
Stir in beaten egg yolks and let cool for 5 minutes.

Beat 3 egg whites until stiff. Fold in chopped nuts and whipping cream.
Then fold into the chocolate mixture.

Crumble 1 large angel food cake and put half of the crumbs in a 9 x 12
rectangular pan. Pour half of the chocolate mixture over the cake. Add other
layer of the cake crumbs and remaining chocolate mixture. Place in
refrigerator to set. Serves 15.

Chocolate Pudding Cake ... warm pudding & brownies

1 c flour   ½ c milk
¾ c sugar   2 T melted butter
1 T cocoa   1 t vanilla
2 t baking powder   1 c brown sugar
¼ t salt   ¼ c cocoa
¾ chopped nuts   1¾ c boiling water

In a 9-inch square cake pan, mix together the flour, sugar, 2 T cocoa,
baking powder, salt and nuts. Blend in the milk, melted butter and
vanilla. In separate bowl, mix the brown sugar and the ¼ c cocoa and
pour over the flour mixture in the pan. Pour boiling water over all. Bake
at 350 degrees for 50 minutes. Makes 8-10 very rich servings.

*I love this warm pudding cake; brownies on the top and chocolate
pudding on the bottom. Even better with Kool Whip or ice cream topping.*

Tanya's Chocolate Mousse ... cake without flour

11 oz bittersweet chocolate	⅔ c sugar
2 oz milk chocolate	1 T vanilla
¾ c unsalted butter	pinch of salt
8 large eggs, separated	9-inch spring form pan
scant ½ c light brown sugar	heavy-duty aluminum foil

Preheat the oven to 350 degrees and put the kettle on to boil.

Line the inside of the spring form pan with foil, making sure you press the foil well into the sides and bottom of the pan so that it forms a smooth surface. This will prevent water from getting into the cake when it is cooked in its water bath.

Melt the chocolate and butter in a microwave or double boiler, and let it cool. In another bowl, beat the egg yolks and sugars until very thick and pale, as creamy as mayonnaise: the mixture should form and fall in ribbons when you lift up the whisk. Stir in the vanilla and salt, and then the cooled chocolate mixture. Whisk the egg whites in a large bowl until soft peaks form, then lighten the chocolate mixture with a briskly beaten-in dollop of whites before gently folding the rest of them into it.

Pour the cake batter into the foil-lined spring form pan, which you have placed in a large roasting pan. Add hot water from the recently boiled kettle to come about 1 inch up the sides of the cake pan and carefully put the roasting pan with its cargo into the oven.

Cook for 50 minutes-1 hour. The inside of the cake will be damp and mousse-like, but the top should look cooked and dry. Let it cool completely on a cooling rack before releasing it from the pan. This calls for a little bit of patience, because you will need to peel the foil gently away from the sides. Just go slowly and remember that this is a very damp cake, and you won't be able to pry it away from its foil-lined base-though it's easy enough to tear off excess foil once you've set the cake on its plate. For a finishing touch, dust with confectioner's sugar, and serve with crème fraiche*, and/or maybe some raspberries. Serves 6-8.

Crème fraîche is a slightly tangy, slightly nutty, thickened cream.

Chocolate Almond-Torte

1 pkg chocolate cake mix
1⅓ c slivered almonds
½ c sugar
1 small pkg vanilla instant pudding

1¼ c milk
¾ t almond extract
1½ c Kool Whip
1 tub prepared chocolate frosting

Heat oven to 350 degrees. Bake cake in two 9-inch pans as directed on pkg. Cool 10 minutes; remove from pans and cool completely. Split cake to make four layers. Cook almonds and sugar over medium heat, stirring constantly, until sugar is melted and almonds are coated. Spread on wax paper. Cool and break apart. Mix pudding, milk, and almond extract until smooth and well blended. Fold in Kool Whip. Spread ¼ of the pudding mixture and ¼ of the almonds between layers and on top of torte. Frost sides of torte with chocolate frosting. Refrigerate two to three hours before serving. Refrigerate remaining torte.

This torte was brought to a church meeting by a friend of mine, and I have never seen so many men stand around, and lick a cake plate like they did that night!

Chocolate Cake … the old way

Cake:
2 c sugar
2 c flour
½ c buttermilk
½ t soda
1 stick butter
½ c shortening
4 T cocoa
1 c water
2 eggs
1 t vanilla

Icing:
1 stick butter, melted
4 T cocoa
6 T milk

1 box powdered sugar
1 t vanilla
1 c chopped pecans

Sift sugar and flour together and stir in buttermilk, soda, eggs and vanilla. In a saucepan mix butter, shortening, cocoa and water and bring to a boil. Pour over sugar-flour mixture and mix. Pour batter into a sheet cake pan and bake at 350 degrees for 35 minutes. Ice while still warm.

To prepare icing bring milk, butter, and cocoa to a boil. Remove from heat and stir in powdered sugar, vanilla and pecans.

Earthquake Chocolate Cake ... rich and delicious

1 box German chocolate cake mix
1 3½-oz can sweetened flaked
   coconut
1 c chopped nuts
¼ c margarine

8 oz cream cheese, softened
16-oz box powdered sugar
Kool Whip

Prepare cake batter according to package instructions. Preheat oven to 350 degrees. Grease a 9 x 12 inch baking pan. Cover the bottom of the pan with the nuts and coconut. Pour cake batter on top. Melt margarine in a bowl. Add the cream cheese and powdered sugar. Stir to blend. Spoon over unbaked batter and bake for 40-42 minutes. You can't test for doneness with this sticky cake.   Serve in bowls with Kool whip and chocolate chips on top.

Quick Chocolate Frosting

When you don't have time to make icing from scratch, blend a half can of chocolate frosting with 3 ounces of softened cream cheese in a mixing bowl. The creamy result is not as sweet or as thick as the cooked icing, but it is very good.

Coal Miner's Cake

1 box Devil's Food cake mix
1 can cherry pie filling

2 eggs
1 t vanilla

Preheat oven to 350 degrees. Mix all ingredients and bake in a 9 x 13 pan for 30 to 35 minutes. While cake is still hot, cover with topping

Topping:
1 c sugar
1 stick margarine
¼ c evaporated milk

6-oz pkg chocolate chips
½ c pecans or walnuts, chopped

In saucepan, warm mixture of sugar, margarine and evaporated milk over low heat. Bring to low boil for one minute; add chocolate chips and nuts and stir until melted. Pour over cake.

Coconut-Topped Brownie Cake

Make 1 pkg brownies according to directions on box and cook in a 13 x 9 inch pan.

Coconut topping:
2 7-oz bags shredded coconut
1 cup sweetened condensed milk
2 large egg whites

1 T flour
1½ t vanilla extract
⅛ t baking powder

To make coconut topping: combine all ingredients in a large bowl. Stir to combine. Remove brownies from oven (after 20 minutes of baking); spoon coconut mixture evenly over top. Return to oven and bake until tips of coconut are golden brown, 25 to 30 minutes more. Serves 30.

Cottage Pudding

¾ c sugar
¼ c butter or margarine
1 egg
1 c self-rising flour
½ c milk
1 t vanilla

Vanilla Cream Sauce:
½ c sugar
1 c boiling water
1 T butter or margarine(use more
    for a richer sauce)
1½ T flour
1 t vanilla or 1 T for richer flavor

Cream butter with mixer, add sugar and blend, then add the egg and blend well. Add sifted flour to mixture, alternately with the milk until smooth.

Fill greased muffin tins ¾ full and bake in 350 degree oven for about 20 minutes or until muffins are done. They should be slightly browned and are done when an inserted toothpick comes out clean. Serve warm with vanilla sauce.

To make sauce: Mix flour into sugar and gradually add to boiling water, constantly stirring. Boil five minutes or until slightly thickened. Remove from range and stir in butter and vanilla.

Cheesy Fruity Cupcakes ... quick and easy

1 pkg cake mix
1 8-oz pkg cream cheese, softened

¼ c preserves
1 can of cake frosting

Make cake mix according to pkg directions. Fill 18 cup cakes, half way.
Mix preserves and cream cheese and add a dollop to each cup cake. Cook
for 325 degrees according to box. Ice with can of frosting.

Creamsicle Cake ... tastes just like the orange treat

18-25 oz orange cake mix*
2 3-oz pkgs orange Jell-o
3 pkg instant vanilla pudding

1 c milk
1 t vanilla
8 oz Kool whip

Bake cake as directed in a 9 x 13 inch pan. When done, use a meat fork
to poke holes across the top of the entire cake. Let cool.

In bowl, mix one box jell-o with one cup of hot water. Add one cup of
cold water. Pour over top of cake. Refrigerate for two or three hours.

Mix remaining box of jell-o, pudding mix, milk, and vanilla together.
Beat well. Fold Kool whip into this mixture and spread on top of cake.
Keep refrigerated.

*If you cannot find an orange cake mix, use a lemon cake mix and add
one small envelop of orange Kool Aid to the batter.*

Cream Cheese Pound Cake

1 c margarine, softened
½ c butter, softened (do not
    substitute)
8 oz cream cheese, softened

3 cups sugar
6 eggs
3 cups flour
2 t vanilla

Combine first 3 ingredients, creaming well. Gradually add sugar, beating
until light and fluffy. Add eggs, one at a time, beating well after each
addition. Add flour to creamed mixture, stirring until combined. Stir in
vanilla. Pour batter into a well-greased 10-inch tube pan. Bake at 325
degrees for 1 hour and 45 minutes or until cake test done. Cool in pan 10
minutes, remove from pan, and cool completely.

Cupcakes ... low fat and low sugar

1 chocolate cake mix
1 can diet cola

1 lemon cake mix
1 can of diet Sprite

Choose either combination of cake mixes and cola, and combine. Fill paper baking cups in muffin tins half full with batter. Bake according to directions on cake mix box. Cool and serve with a dollop of fat free Kool Whip.

Dump Cake ... never a bite left

1 can cherry pie filling
8¼-oz can crushed pineapple,
    do not drain
1 yellow cake mix

2 sticks butter, melted
2½-oz can flaked coconut
1 c chopped pecans
Kool Whip for topping

Spoon cherry pie filling evenly in bottom of large sheet cake pan. Spread pineapple over cherry pie filling. Sprinkle dry cake mix over pineapple, then sprinkle coconut and finally pecans. Pour melted butter over the top and bake at 350 degrees for about 55 minutes until golden brown.

Easy, quick, and very good. Can mix when beginning dinner and have ready in time for dessert.

Flop Cake

1 yellow cake mix
1 egg
1 stick butter, melted
8 oz cream cheese, softened

1 box powdered sugar
2 eggs
your favorite caramel frosting

Mix cake mix, one egg and butter together in a sheet cake pan. Spread evenly over bottom of pan. Mix cream cheese, powdered sugar and 2 eggs together with a blender and pour over mixture in pan. Bake at 350 degrees for 35 to 40 minutes. Frost cake with your favorite caramel frosting.

Cushaw or Pumpkin Cake

1 c oil
4 eggs
2 c sugar
2 c flour
½ t salt
2 t soda
2 t baking powder
1 t cinnamon

1 t vanilla
½ c chopped nuts
2 c cooked cushaw or pumpkin

Icing:
8 oz cream cheese, softened
½ c softened butter
2 t milk
5¾ - 6¼ c powdered sugar

Cream oil, eggs and sugar. Mix flour, salt, soda, baking powdered and cinnamon. Blend into egg mixture and add vanilla, nuts and cushaw.

Pour into a greased and floured Bundt pan. Bake for 1 hour at 350 degrees. When cool, frost with cream cheese icing.

To make cream cheese icing: Beat softened cream cheese, butter, and milk until light and fluffy. Gradually add powdered sugar, 2 cups at a time until spreading consistency.

Cushaws are large crook-neck squashes, usually green and white striped, harvested in the Fall. They are as good, if not better than pumpkins, and can be cooked in the microwave, by slicing in half and baking each half for about 20 minutes until done. Pulp can be scraped out and frozen for future use.

Fudge Cake ... Soccer Mom style

1 small pkg chocolate pudding
    (cook and serve kind)
2 c milk

1 box chocolate cake mix
1 c chocolate chips
½ c chopped nuts

Cook pudding and milk as directed on package. Blend dry cake mix into hot pudding. Pour into 9 x 13 pan. Sprinkle chocolate chips and nuts on top. Bake 350 degrees for 30-35 minutes. Serve warm with Kool Whip topping.

Fruitcake ... fantastic

3 c flour
¼ t baking soda
1 t salt
1 t baking powder
1 t cinnamon
½ t nutmeg
½ t allspice
2 c sugar

1 c shortening
1½ c applesauce
1½ c canned peach slices, chopped
   and drained
1 c light raisins
1 c dark raisins
½ c maraschino cherries, cut in half
1 c shredded coconut
2 c chopped pecans

Preheat oven to 300 degrees. Plump raisins for 1 minute in 1 cup boiling water; drain and set aside. Sift together first 7 ingredients and set aside. Cream sugar and shortening with blender. Add remaining ingredients including raisins, to sugar mixture, stirring well after each addition. Add flour mixture and cream well with wooden spoon. Pour into greased and floured large bundt or loaf pan. Bake 2½ to 3 hours until tooth pick inserted in center comes out clean. Serves 16.

German Chocolate Cake with Coconut Icing

1 German chocolate cake mix

Icing:
⅔ c sugar
⅔ c evaporated milk
2 egg yolks, slightly beaten

1⅓ c flaked coconut
⅔-1 c chopped pecans
⅓ c butter
½ t vanilla

Prepare cake mix according to package directions in two 8-inch pans. Cool cake.

To make icing: Combine all except the coconut and nuts in a pan. Cook and stir constantly over medium heat about 10 minutes or until the egg thickens. Remove from heat and add coconut and pecans.

Never-Fail Chocolate Icing ... a must-have recipe

1 c granulated sugar
½ c water
6 T cocoa
pinch of salt

1 t vanilla
½ stick butter
1 box powdered sugar, or more

Mix and heat granulated sugar, water, cocoa and salt until it come to a boil. Boil for 1 minute only. Remove from heat and add butter and vanilla. Beat and gradually add enough powdered sugar until spreading consistency is reached. May add a touch of milk if icing becomes too hard or too thick.

May also make an excellent *caramel icing* from the above recipe by substituting brown sugar for white sugar and omitting the chocolate. This recipe will work for any amount as along as a 2:1 ratio of sugar to water is used.

Brown Sugar Icing

1 c brown sugar
1 stick butter (7 T)

¼ c milk
1 t vanilla

Mix sugar, butter and milk in 1 quart saucepan. Bring to a boil. Boil for 4 minutes. Remove from heat. Stir in vanilla. Stir. Thickens as it cools.

Cream Cheese Chocolate Icing ... a classic

3 oz cream cheese
¼ c milk
3 c powdered sugar

⅛ t salt
1 t vanilla
3 sq melted chocolate

Blend all ingredients in bowl with mixer. Blend in melted chocolate until desired spreading consistency.

Hummingbird Cake ... a prize winner

1 yellow cake mix
1 t cinnamon
3 eggs, beaten
½ c oil
1½ t vanilla
18-oz can crushed pineapple
2 c chopped walnuts
2 c bananas, mashed

Cream Cheese Frosting
½ c butter, softened
8-oz pkg cream cheese
1 lb powdered sugar
1 T vanilla

Preheat oven to 350 degrees. Make the cake first, combining mix and cinnamon in a large bowl. Add eggs and oil, stirring by hand until dry ingredients are moistened. Stir in vanilla, pineapple, bananas and one cup of crushed walnuts. Stir only with a spoon. Do not use an electric mixer. Spoon batter into three well-greased and floured round cake pans. Bake until cake is done (about 28-30 minutes). Cool in pans for 10 minutes.

Remove cakes from pans and cool on wire rack. Meanwhile, make the frosting by beating butter and cream cheese with an electric mixer until light and fluffy. Add powdered sugar gradually, beating until spreading consistency. Beat in vanilla. Frost each layer, and top with next layer. Finish frosting cake and sprinkle remaining chopped walnuts on top.

Jam Cake for Busy Cooks

1 box spice cake mix
3 eggs
1 c water

⅓ c oil
1 c blackberry jam
½ c chopped pecans

Preheat oven to 350 degrees. Add eggs, oil and water to dry cake mix. Mix according to directions on box. Add blackberry jam and nuts and beat only long enough to mix thoroughly. Pour mixture into greased and floured 9 x 13 x 2 inch pan. Bake for 35 minutes or until cake begins to pull from sides of pan and toothpick inserted comes out clean. Cool in pan on rack. Ice with *Never Fail Caramel Icing*.

Never-Fail Caramel Icing

1 c brown sugar
½ c water
Pinch of salt

1 t vanilla
½ stick butter
1 box powdered sugar, or more

Mix and heat granulated sugar, water, and salt until it come to a boil. Boil for 1 minute only. Remove from heat and add butter and vanilla. Beat and gradually add enough powdered sugar until spreading consistency is reached. May add a touch of milk if icing becomes too hard or too thick.

Mary's Old Kentucky Black Walnut Jam Cake

2 c sugar
1 t soda
1 c butter or margarine
2 t cinnamon
1 t nutmeg
3 eggs, separated
1 c blackberry jam
1 c raisins
3 c flour
1 c black walnuts

Icing:
3 c brown sugar
1 c nuts, chopped
2 c cream or whole milk
pinch of salt
1 t vanilla
2 T butter

Cream butter and sugar until light and fluffy. Separate eggs and beat the egg yolks well, add butter and sugar mixture. Add jam. Sift the flour, salt, soda, cinnamon and nutmeg and add to the mixture. Fold in beaten egg whites.

Line two large cake pans or three small ones with heavily greased and floured wax paper. Bake in a preheated oven at 325 degrees until cake pulls away from the side of the pans about 45-60 minutes. Cool on wire racks. When cool remove waxed paper, and frost.

To make frosting, cook the milk and brown sugar until it forms a soft ball when a few drops are dropped into a cup of cold water. Remove from the heat, add the vanilla and butter. Beat with a mixer until the frosting is of spreading consistency. Add the nuts and spread between the layers, and on the sides and top of the cake.

Lemon Pudding Cake

5 level t flour	¼ c lemon juice, 2 lemons
1 c sugar	¼ t grated lemon rind
3 T butter, softened or melted	3 eggs, separated
1 c milk	

Mix flour and sugar; work butter into flour mixture and cream. Beat egg yolks until thick and lemon colored. Add yolks and milk to creamed mixture. Mix. Gradually add lemon juice and rind, and mix carefully. Beat egg whites until stiff, but not dry; fold into mixture carefully. Pour into a greased 8-9-inch baking dish. Set dish in a pan containing about one inch of hot water; place in 350 degree oven and bake about 35 minutes or until set. Serves six.

Delicious . . . cake on top and lemon pudding on the bottom. I serve it warm.

Susan's Midnight Bliss Chocolate Cake … fantastic!

1 pkg devil's food cake mix	4 eggs
1 pkg Jell-O instant chocolate pudding mix	½ c oil
	8 oz sour cream
½ c General Mills International coffee (Mocha Swiss Powder)	½ c water
	12-oz pkg mini chocolate chips

Preheat oven 350 degrees. Grease Bundt Pan. Beat all ingredients except chocolate chips at low speed until moistened. Beat at medium speed for 2 minutes. Stir in Chocolate pieces. Bake 60 minutes until toothpick comes out clean. Cool in pan for 20-30 minutes. Turn upside down on plate and continue cooling. When completely cooled, sprinkle with powdered sugar.

Absolutely fantastic chocolate cake…. Moist and no need to ice...; doesn't last long at our house; the family slivers it to death! --One of my husband's favorites. Can make combinations of other ingredients i.e. yellow cake, butterscotch pudding and vanilla chips.

Mississippi Mud Cake

2 c sugar
4 eggs, whole
⅓ c cocoa
1 t vanilla
3 sticks butter
1½ c flour
1⅓ c coconut
½ c pecans
jar of marshmallow cream

Icing:
1 box powdered sugar
1 c milk
¼ lb. butter
⅓ c cocoa

Mix sugar, eggs, cocoa, vanilla and butter. Add. flour, coconut and pecans and mix well and bake in a greased 11x 13 pan at 350 degrees for 35 minutes. Spread marshmallow cream on top while cake is still hot.

Melt butter; add sugar, milk and cocoa. Mix well and pour on cake.

Heath Bar Cake, a.k.a. *Holy Cow Cake*

1 German Chocolate cake mix
8 oz Kool Whip
1 can Eagle Brand Milk
1 jar regular caramel ice cream
   topping
4 Heath bars

Prepare cake in greased 9 x 13 inch pan and cool. Poke numerous holes in cake with fork. Pour 1 can of Eagle Brand milk over the cake, letting it settle into holes. Cool completely in refrigerator. Top with Kool Whip. Break up the 4 Heath Bars into small pieces, and sprinkle on top. Store cake in refrigerator.

Punch Bowl Cake ... great, quick and easy

1 Jiffy cake mix, prepared
1 large vanilla pudding, prepared
bananas
chopped nuts
1 can crushed pineapple, drained
1 can cherry pie filling
Kool Whip

Crumble prepared cake into a big, clear bowl. Layer rest of ingredients and cool.

Peaches and Pecan Sandies Dessert

1 bag Pecan Sandies cookies
7 T butter, melted
8 oz cream cheese, softened
1 c powdered sugar
8 oz Kool Whip

10 oz clear cola
4 T cornstarch
1 c sugar
3 T peach jello
6-8 peaches, peeled and sliced

Crush cookies into small bits, and add melted butter. Press into 9 x 13 inch pyrex pan. Bake for 10 minutes at 325 degrees. Blend cream cheese, powdered sugar and Kool Whip. Spread over cooled crust. Bring cola, cornstarch, sugar and jello to a boil. Boil 4 minutes, and then cool. Add sliced peaches. Spread over cream cheese mixture and chill.

Mountain Dew Cupcakes

½ c chopped pecans for
    lining muffin cups
1 box yellow cake mix with
    pudding in the mix
1 box instant vanilla pudding

½ c Mountain Dew
½ c oil
½ c water
4 eggs

Line muffin tins with papers and sprinkle with pecans. Mix cake mix with rest of the ingredients and spoon into cups. Fill half way. Cook for 50-60 minutes at 350 degrees.

Icing:

1 stick butter
¼ c Mountain Dew

1¾ c sugar
3½ oz coconut

Mix ingredients and bring to a boil. Boil for 2 minutes. Pour over cupcakes while warm.

Mountain Pudding Cake ... easy peach cobbler
Melt ¾ stick of butter in 13 x 9 cake pan in a 350-degree oven.

Make batter of:
1 c flour
1 c sugar
1½ t baking powder
¼ t salt
¾ c milk
1 large can peaches, sliced

Mix first 5 ingredients, quickly and pour batter into pan. Let cover bottom of pan. Pour peaches with juice over top of the batter. Bake at 350 degrees for about one hour. Last 5 minutes, butter top of cake and sprinkle with sugar. Serve as is, or with ice cream.

Can put this in the oven when you start dinner and it will be done by the time everything else is ready. Can do this with can of pie cherries, too.

Oatmeal Coconut Cake ... an oldie, but goodie
1 c quick cooking oats
1 stick butter
1 c white sugar
1 c brown sugar
2 eggs
1 t cinnamon
1½ c sifted flour
1 t soda
½ t salt
1 t nutmeg
1 t ground cloves

Pour 1¼ cup boiling water over 1 cup quick cooking oats and 1 stick butter. Let stand for 20 minutes.
Add remaining ingredients to oatmeal mixture and bake for 35 minutes at 350 degrees in a 1 x 13 inch greased Pyrex dish.

Topping:
½ c margarine
3 T milk
1 c nuts
1 c coconut
1 c brown sugar

Mix and pour over hot cake and put under broiler for 2 minutes or until lightly browned.

Mildred's Pig Lickin' Cake ... an oldie and goodie

1 box (18¼ oz) yellow cake mix
4 eggs
1 t butter flavoring, optional
1 t vanilla
1 can (11 oz.) mandarin oranges,
   undrained
½ c vegetable oil
1 c chopped nuts (optional)

Frosting:
1 carton (9 oz.) frozen non-dairy
   whipped topping, thawed
1 box (4-serving size) instant
   vanilla pudding
1 can (20 oz.) crushed pineapple,
   partially drained.

Mix cake mix, eggs, butter flavoring if desired, vanilla, oranges and liquid and the oil together. Pour into greased and floured 13x9-inch pan or 2 round layer pans. Bake at 350 degrees for 35 minutes or until toothpick inserted in center comes out clean. Cool on wire rack. Mix together all ingredients of frosting and spread on cooled cake and refrigerate.

Pineapple Upside Down Cake ... the easy way

2 T butter
1 Jiffy cake mix
small can pineapple rings

1 c brown sugar
maraschino cherries

Heat butter and brown sugar in a cast iron skillet on the stove until sugar is melted. Remove from heat and add pineapples and several cherries in the center of pineapple circles. Mix cake mix according to directions on package and pour in skillet. Bake at 350 degrees for 30 minutes. Turn upside down on plate to cool.

Some More S'Mores, Please

One of my favorite childhood memories is of summer campfires and roasted marshmallows. My fondness for that tradition as a child may have been partially due the permitted "playing with fire." In any event, the campfire meant fun and the excitement of the mystery in the darkness just outside that circle of light. I developed great skill in the roasting of each marshmallow to just the right shade of golden brown, melting it to the proper consistency without burning it. I thought there could be nothing better than a roasted marshmallow, until the evening my aunt brought Hershey's candy bars and graham crackers to the campfire.

When she added the chocolate and graham cracker to my roasted marshmallow I couldn't believe how good it was. The Girl Scouts had first recorded the recipe for this delicacy which they called "S'Mores" in 1927. And now, I had my very first dessert recipe. From then on, we never had a campfire without S'Mores.

As I grew older, campfires became more infrequent, but I would often fondly remember them and the wonderful S'Mores. When my own children began to go to church summer camp I was asked to go along as counselor. It was there at snack time in the camp kitchen that I first saw the mass production of S'Mores. Amazingly, it was possible for the kids to enjoy S'Mores without what I, as an adult, considered the inconvenience of a campfire in the backyard.

To make S'Mores in the kitchen

Place graham cracker squares on a cookie sheet. Place half of a Hershey's bar, then a marshmallow on top of each. Cook in a 400 degree oven for about five minutes. Remove from the oven and press another graham cracker square on top of each marshmallow. Cool slightly and enjoy while warm.

During sweet-treat emergencies, this can also be done in the microwave. Heat for 10-15 seconds only. It's fun for the kids to watch the marshmallows inflate while cooking. Careful – they're hot when they come out of the microwave.

Popovers ... a favorite from Maine

3 eggs
1 c milk
1 c flour
½ t salt
2 T melted butter or margarine

Filling:
1 large instant vanilla pudding
3 c milk

Grease muffin tins and place them in oven preheated to 450 degrees. Beat eggs well and add milk and butter. Mix flour and salt and add to liquid and beat until smooth. Fill muffin cups ¾ full of batter. Bake for 15 minutes at 450 degrees, and then reduce heat to 375 degrees and bake 10 minutes longer until golden brown. Insert a sharp knife into each to allow steam to escape. This allows popovers to keep their shape. Use plain with butter or make pudding according to directions on box and fill the popovers. Cool and store in refrigerator.

Can fill with cherry pie filling or your favorite filling.

Rum Cake ... very good

½ c chopped pecans
1 Duncan Hines Butter Recipe
   Golden Cake Mix
1 small pkg vanilla instant pudding

4 eggs
½ c water
½ c oil
½ c light rum

Grease and flour a bundt pan. Crumble nuts in bottom of pan. Place cake mix and pudding mix in large bowl. Add rum, water, oil and eggs. Mix for six minutes. Pour batter into cake pan and bake 50-60 minutes at 325 degrees. Remove from oven and immediately pour on hot glaze. Let cool in Bundt pan until it is completely cool. Wrap tightly.

Hot Glaze:
1 c sugar
1 stick butter
¼ c light rum
¼ c water

Mix ingredients, boil 2-3 minutes
and pour over cake

Pinwheel Cake ... an old, family treat

Melt:
4 1-oz sq unsweetened chocolate

Sift:
1¾ sifted flour
1½ c sugar
2 t baking powder
¼ t soda
1 t salt
Stir: ½ c shortening to soften and
add sifted ingredients

Add:
1¼ c evaporated milk, divided
1 t vanilla
Mix to dampen flour. Beat 2
minutes at low speed of mixer.

Add:
2 eggs
¼ c evaporated milk
melted chocolate squares

Melt 2 sq of chocolate; sift together flour, sugar, baking powder, soda and
salt. Stir shortening and mix with chocolate; add to sifted ingredients.
Add evaporated milk, vanilla and mix to dampen flour. Beat two minutes
at low speed with mixer. Add eggs and ¼ cup of evaporated milk. Beat
1 minute. Pour batter into two 9 inch layer pans, lined on the bottom with
waxed paper.

Melt 2 more squares of chocolate. Pour in a circle on top of batter in each
pan, about 1 inch from rim. With a rubber scrapper, swirl the chocolate in
continuous circles, once around the rim. Bake at 350 degrees about 30
minutes . Cool and split to make four layers. Spread "Fluffy Chocolate
Filling" between layers. Chill before serving.

Fluffy Chocolate Filling

1 sq unsweetened chocolate melted
   and cooled
⅔ c vegetable shortening
½ c sugar

⅓ c evaporated milk
1 T water
¼ t salt
1 t vanilla

Beat on high with mixer 10 minutes or until fluffy.

Strawberry Cake ... an oldie, but goodie

1 pkg white cake mix
4 eggs
1 pkg strawberry Jell-O

1 c oil
1 c drained frozen strawberries
(save juice)

Pour all but berries in mixer bowl and beat about 4 minutes. Add berries. Pour into large greased Pyrex casserole dish. Bake for 35 minutes at 325 degrees

Frosting:

¾ stick margarine
1 box powdered sugar
strawberry juice

Mix butter and sugar and as much liquid as needed to make spreading consistency.

Sandy's Pumpkin Roll ... fantastic and terrific!

3 eggs
1 c sugar
1 t lemon juice
1 t soda
¼ t salt
1 t ginger
1 t allspice
½ t nutmeg
¾ c flour
⅔ c pumpkin

Filling:
1 c powdered sugar
¼ c soft margarine
8 oz cream cheese
2 t vanilla

Grease a cookie sheet with a lip with Pam and line with waxed paper and heavily grease the waxed paper again. Beat eggs, sugar and lemon juice. Combine soda, salt, ginger, allspice, nutmeg, and flour and fold into eggs.

Add pumpkin and stir. Spread the batter in the prepared cookie sheet. Bake for 20 minutes at 350 degrees or until slightly browned. Turn out on a towel covered with powdered sugar and remove waxed paper from back. Roll up long ways with the towel in a jellyroll manner. Cool in the towel for 2 hours. Unroll, and spread with filling; re-roll without the towel.

Wrap in waxed paper and then in Reynolds Wrap. Refrigerate and slice as needed. Freezes well.

This is great and everyone loves it!. We even use it for breakfast. It takes quite a bit of preparation, but it is well worth it.

Easy Tiramisu

10¾ oz frozen pound cake, thawed
¾ c strong brewed coffee
8 oz cream cheese, softened
1 c sugar

½ c chocolate syrup
1 c Kool Whip
2 Heath candy bars (1.4 oz each),
   crushed

Cut cake into nine slices. Arrange in an un-greased 11 x 7 x 2 in dish, cutting to fit if needed. Drizzle with coffee. In a small mixing bowl, beat the cream cheese until smooth. Add the chocolate syrup. Fold in Kool Whip and spread over cake. Sprinkle with crushed candy bars. Refrigerate. Serves 8.

Red Velvet Cake … an old, family treat

3 T cocoa, heaping
small bottle red cake coloring, then
   fill bottle with water
2 beaten eggs
½ c sugar
½ c shortening

2¼ sifted cake flour
1 c buttermilk
1 t vanilla
1 t soda
1 T vinegar
½ t salt

Preheat oven to 350 degrees. Prepare two 9 inch round cake pans with waxed paper. Make a paste by combining cocoa and cake coloring and water. Cream eggs, sugar, shortening, and add to paste. To this add the salt, buttermilk, and vanilla. Dissolve soda in the vinegar and add while foaming to cake batter. Bake at 350 degrees for 35-40 minutes. Remove from pan after 10 minutes. Cool. Split to make 4 layers.

Icing:
7½ T flour
1½ c milk
1½ c sugar

1½ c margarine
1 t vanilla

Add milk to flour slowly. Cook on low heat until they form a paste. Cool completely. Beat sugar and margarine with mixer until light. Add paste. Ice between layers and on top.

You can make 1⅓ icing recipe and ice sides of cake, too.

Charlene's Thanksgiving Cake

18 oz pkg spice cake mix	3 eggs
1 c canned pumpkin	1 t cinnamon
½ c salad oil	½ c water
1 sm box instant vanilla pudding	½ c pecans, chopped

Mix all ingredients, except nuts, and beat at medium speed for 5 minutes, then add nuts. Grease a bundt pan liberally. Sprinkle with flour. Pour batter into pan and bake at 350 degrees for 45 to 55 minutes or until a toothpick comes out clean from the middle of the cake. Let cool in pan for 15 minutes. Loosen center and sides of the cake. Invert on wire rack to cool. Serve with Kool whip.

Turtle Sundae Dessert ... an easy chocolate treat

1 German chocolate cake mix	1 c chopped nuts
14 oz pkg caramels	1 cup chocolate chips
½ c evaporated milk	*optional:*
6 T butter or margarine	vanilla ice cream and pecan halves

Mix the cake according to package directions. Set aside half of the batter, pour remaining batter into a greased and floured 13 x 9 x 2 inch baking pan. Bake at 350 degrees for 18 minutes. Meanwhile, in a saucepan over low heat, melt the caramels, milk and butter. Remove from the heat and add nuts. Pour over cake. Sprinkle with chocolate chips. Pour the reserved batter over the top. Bake 20-25 minutes more or until cake springs back when lightly touched. Cool. Cut into squares. If desired, top each square with a scoop of ice cream and a pecan half. Serves: 20.

White Chocolate Cheesecake with Chocolate Crust

Crust:
2 c oreo crumbs
4 T butter
Cheesecake:
1 c sugar

2 pounds cream cheese, room
temperature
1 t vanilla
4 eggs
8 oz white chocolate, melted

Mix Oreo crumbs with butter and press into the bottom of a spring form pan. Cream sugar and cream cheese together. Add vanilla. Add eggs one at a time and continue beating. Blend in chocolate. Pour into crust and place spring form in a water bath. (Place the cake mix in a baking dish large enough to accommodate it, and add enough hot water to reach halfway up the sides of the pan.)
Bake at 450 degrees for 20 minutes. Reduce heat to 250 degrees and continue to bake for 1 hour or until firm. Cool thoroughly, overnight, before removing from pan. Serve with pureed raspberries, sweetened to taste with honey or sugar.

Twinkie Delight

1 box Twinkies
2 small boxes butter pecan
    instant pudding

8 oz Kool Whip
1 Heath candy bar, crushed

Cut Twinkies in half lengthwise and place in an 11 x 7 glass dish or pan. Make pudding as directed on box and pour over the Twinkies. Spread Kool Whip on top and top with crushed Heath Bars. Refrigerate. Serves 8 -12.

Margaret's Wacky Cake

1½ c flour
1 c sugar
3 T Hershey's Cocoa powder
1 t soda
½ t salt

1 T vinegar
1 c cold water
6 T melted margarine or oil
1 T vanilla

Sift all dry ingredients into an un-greased 9 inch baking dish. Punch 3 holes in the mixture. Into the largest hole pour the margarine, into the middle sized hole pour the vinegar and into the smallest, pour the vanilla. Over these ingredients pour the water. Stir well with a fork and bake at 350 degrees for 25 minutes. You can ice the cake in the pan or serve it with *Chocolate Sauce*.

Put in small heavy saucepan:
2 T butter
½ c cocoa
Stir over low heat until the
    chocolate melts.

Add:
1 c sugar
few grains salt
½ c water

Cook, stirring constantly until the sauce is as thick as you like. Add a teaspoon of vanilla.

Woodford Pudding

½ c butter
1 c sugar
1 c flour
1 c blackberry jam

1 t baking powder
½ c milk
1 t cinnamon
3 eggs, beaten

Cream butter and sugar; add eggs. Add flour sifted with cinnamon and baking powder to the sugar and egg mixture along with the milk. Blend in the jam. Bake in greased dish about 8 x 12 for 40 minutes at 325 degrees. Serve with *Caramel Sauce*:

1½ c brown sugar
dash salt

1 c boiling water
4 T flour

Blend sugar, salt and flour and add boiling water in a sauce pan. Stir and cool 6-8 minutes. If too thick, may add more water. Take off stove and add 4 T butter and ½ t vanilla.

Walnut Cake with Lemon Filling ... a special treat

1 yellow cake mix
½ c chopped walnuts
1 can lemon pie filling
1 egg white
¾ c sugar

⅛ t cream of tartar
3 T water
½ t vanilla
whole walnuts for topping

Prepare cake mix according to package directions; add walnuts and bake in 2 round 9 inch cake pans that have been sprayed with Pam and lined with waxed paper. When cake is cool, place one layer on plate and half of lemon pie filling on top. Top with second layer and frost with *Double Boiler Frosting*. Garnish with walnuts

Double Boiler Frosting

Mix in top of double boiler egg white, sugar, cream of tartar, and water. Place over boiling water and beat with mixer until mixture holds its shape, about 7 minutes. Fold in vanilla. Remove from heat and continue beating until cool and stiff.

This old family cake was originally made from scratch and I upgraded it with a cake mix and a can of lemon pie filling.

Blueberry or Blackberry Cheesecake

6 T butter or margarine, melted
2 c graham cracker crumbs
2 8-oz pkgs Philadelphia cream
   cheese, softened

¾ c sugar
2 large eggs
1 t vanilla
8 oz jar blueberry or blackberry
   jam
1 c blueberries or blackberries

Preheat oven to 350 degrees. Melt butter into a 9 x 13-inch baking pan. Sprinkle crumbs over butter; mix well. Press firmly and evenly into bottom of pan.

Beat cream cheese until smooth. Add sugar, eggs and vanilla, beating until well blended. Set aside. Stir jam in jar until softened. Spread jam evenly over crust; sprinkle with berries. Top with cream cheese mixture.

Bake 30 minutes or until slightly puffed. Cool completely in pan. Refrigerate leftovers.

To soften cream cheese, place unwrapped 8 oz pkg in microwave-able bowl. Microwave on HIGH for 15 seconds. Add 15 seconds for each additional package of cream cheese.

It will be fun in the end. If it's
not fun, it's not the end
— Unknown

Cookies and Brownies

Apple Cookies ... one of my favorites

½ c shortening
1⅓ c brown sugar
1 unbeaten egg
2 c flour
1 t soda
½ t salt
1 t cinnamon

½ t nutmeg
1 c chopped nuts
1 c finely chopped un-pared
    tart apples
1 c raisins
¼ c apple juice or milk

Let raisins stand in hot water until ready to use, then strain. Cream shortening and sugar. Add egg and mix well. Sift dry ingredients and add to mixture. Fold in apples, raisins and nuts. Add juice or milk and mix well. Drop by teaspoons on greased cookie sheet and bake at 350 degrees.

Glaze:
Mix together 1½ c sifted powdered sugar, 1T soft butter, ¼ t vanilla, ⅛ t salt and 2½ T milk.

Blackberry-Sage Thumbprints

2 c flour
⅔ c cornmeal
1½ t dried sage, crushed
¼ t baking powder
1 c butter, softened

1 c packed brown sugar
2 egg yolks
2 t finely shredded lemon peel
1½ t vanilla
¾ c blackberry preserves

Mix flour, cornmeal, sage and baking powder. Set aside. In a large mixing bowl beat butter for 30 seconds with an electric mixer. Add sugar while mixing until combined. Mix in egg yolks, lemon peel, and vanilla. Mix in as much of the flour mixture as possible with the mixer. Stir in any remaining flour mixture. Pinch and roll dough into ¾-inch balls. Place balls one inch apart on an un-greased cookie sheet. With the tip of your thumb indent the top of each ball. Fill the indentation with about ¼ teaspoon of blackberry preserves. Bake about 10 minutes at 350 degrees or until the bottoms are lightly browned. Cool

The first known published recipe for "brownies" appeared in the 1897 *Sears & Roebuck Catalog.*

Dessert Blond Brownies ... a prize winner with ice cream

¾ c butter, softened
2 c packed brown sugar
4 eggs
2 t vanilla
2 c flour
2 t baking powder
1 t salt
1½ c chopped pecans

Maple syrup sauce:
1 c maple syrup
2 T butter
¼ c evaporated milk
vanilla Ice cream
chopped pecans

Cream butter and brown sugar in mixing bowl. Add eggs, one at a time beating well after each addition. Beat in vanilla. Combine the flour, baking soda and salt; gradually add to creamed mixture. Stir in pecans. Spread into a greased 13 x 9 x 2 in baking pan. Bake at 350 degrees for 25-30 minutes or until a toothpick inserted near the center comes out clean. Cool.

Maple Syrup Sauce:
Combine syrup and butter in a saucepan. Bring to a boil; cook and stir for 3 minutes. Remove from the heat; stir in milk. Cut brownies into squares. Place on dessert plates with a scoop of ice cream. Top with sauce; sprinkle with pecans. Makes 20 servings

Cherry Winks ... a Holiday favorite

2 ¼ c flour
1 t baking powder
½ baking soda
½ salt
¾ c shortening or butter
1 c sugar
2 eggs

2 T milk
1 ½ t vanilla
1 c pecans, chopped
1 c dates, pitted and chopped
⅓ c maraschino cherries, cut into
    pieces, divided
2 ½ c corn flakes, crushed

Sift together flour, baking powder, soda and salt. Set aside. Cream shortening and sugar until smooth. Add eggs, milk and vanilla to shortening. Beat until well-mixed. Blend the dry ingredients into egg mixture and continue beating until well blended. Add pecans, dates and cherries. (Reserve some cherries to cut into fourths to place on top of cookies) Mix well.

Roll dough by teaspoons into balls and roll in corn flakes. Place balls on a greased cookie sheet. Top each ball with a piece of cherry. Bake at 375 degrees for 10-12 minutes. Cool on rack before removing.

Chocolate Chip Cheese Bars ... *easy and good*

1 18 oz pkg refrigerated chocolate
    chip cookie dough
½ c sugar

1 egg
8 oz cream cheese, softened

Cut cookie dough in half. For crust, press half of the dough into the bottom of a greased 7-x11 inch baking pan. In a mixing bowl, beat cream cheese, sugar and egg until smooth. Spread over crust. Crumble remaining dough over top. Bake at 350 degrees for 40 minutes or until a toothpick inserted near the center comes out clean. Cool on rack. *Refrigerate, if there are any leftover.*

Chocolate Peanut Bars

1 pkg white cake mix
1⅓ c peanut butter, divided
1 egg
8 oz cream cheese, softened

⅓ c milk
¼ c sugar
1 c chocolate chips
¾ c salted peanuts

In a mixing bowl, beat the cake mix, 1 c peanut butter and egg until crumbly. Press into a greased 13 x 9 baking dish. In a mixing bowl combine cream cheese and remaining peanut butter. Gradually beat in milk and sugar. Carefully spread over crust. Sprinkle with chocolate chips and peanuts. Bake at 350 degrees for 25-30 minutes or until edges are lightly browned and center is set. Cool completely before cutting. Store in the refrigerator. Yield 2 ½ dozen

Chocolate-Coconut Brownies, from a cake mix

1 box chocolate cake mix
1 c flaked coconut

2 eggs
½ c oil

Mix all ingredients together. Pour mixture into a greased and floured 15 x 10 inch pan. Bake at 350 degrees for 15-20 minutes. Cool and cut into squares.

Chocolate Ribbon Bars

11 oz butterscotch chips   ¼ c butter, cubed
1 c peanut butter   2 T water
8 c Rice Krispies cereal   ¾ c powdered sugar
2 c chocolate chips

In a large microwave-safe bowl, melt butterscotch chips and peanut butter; stir until smooth. Gradually stir in cereal until well coated. Press half of the mixture into a greased 13 x 9 2 inch pan; set remaining mixture aside.

In another large microwave-safe bowl, melt chocolate chips and butter. Stir in water until blended. Gradually add the powdered sugar, stirring until smooth. Spread over cereal layer. Cover and refrigerate for 10 minutes or until chocolate layer is set. Spread remaining cereal mixture over the top. Chill before cutting. Makes 24.

Double Chocolate Chip Cookies ... fantastic and easy!

1 pkg. moist devils food cake mix   2 eggs
½ c butter /margarine, softened   ½ c chopped nuts
1 t vanilla   1 c chocolate chips

Preheat oven to 350 degrees. Beat half of dry cake mix, the butter, vanilla, and eggs in large bowl until smooth. STIR in remaining cake mix, nuts, and chocolate chips. Drop dough by rounded teaspoons about 2 inches apart on an un-greased cookie sheet. Bake for 10-12 minutes or until set. Cool 1 minute.

Other combinations are pineapple cake mix and ½ c crushed pineapple or ½ c peanut butter and a yellow cake mix.

Triple Chocolate Brownie Cookies

1 pkg Pillsbury Fudge Supreme
   Walnut Premium Brownie Mix
½ c butter or margarine, melted
1 egg

1 c chocolate-flavored rice crispy
   cereal
1 c chocolate chips
⅔ c quick cooking rolled oats

Heat oven to 350 degrees. In a large bowl, combine brownie mix with nuts, butter and egg; stir with spoon until well blended. Add cereal, chocolate chips and oats; mix well. Drop dough by rounded teaspoonfuls 2 inches apart onto un-greased cookie sheets.

Bake at 350 degrees for 9-12 minutes or until edges are set. (Center will be soft.) Cool 1 minute; remove from cookie sheets. Cool 10 minutes or until completely cooled. Store in tightly covered container. Makes 3½ dozen cookies.

Inez's Fudge Brownies ... brownies from scratch

1 stick butter
1 c sugar
1 16-oz can Hershey's syrup
3 large or 4 small eggs

1¼ c flour
½ t vanilla
½ c chopped nuts
⅛ t salt

Cream margarine and sugar, add eggs and beat, add chocolate syrup, vanilla and flour and mix well. Add nuts last. Bake at 350 degrees in greased 13 x 9 Pyrex dish for 25 minutes. Caution - Do not overcook. Cool in pan for a few minutes. Spread with icing.

Icing:
6 T margarine
6 T milk
1⅓ c sugar
1 T white Karo syrup

1 c chocolate chips
½ c chopped pecans

Place margarine, milk, sugar, and syrup in saucepan and bring to full boil. Boil 1 minute, remove from heat and add chocolate chips. Stir till chips melt, add nuts, and then pour quickly over brownies and spread evenly.

Chocolate Caramel Brownies

1 pkg. (18.25 oz.) chocolate cake
   mix
1 c chopped nuts
1 c evaporated milk, divided

½ c (1 stick) butter or margarine,
   melted
35 caramels (10-oz)
2 c pkg chocolate chips

Preheat oven to 350° F. Combine cake mix and nuts in large bowl. Stir in
⅔ c evaporated milk and butter (batter will be thick). Spread *half* of batter
into un-greased 13 x 9-inch baking pan. Bake for 15 minutes. Heat caramels
and *remaining* evaporated milk in small saucepan over low heat, stirring
constantly, until caramels are melted. Sprinkle morsels over brownies;
drizzle with caramel mixture. Drop *remaining* batter by heaping teaspoon
over caramel mixture. Bake for 25 to 30 minutes or until center is set. Cool
in pan on wire rack.

Chocolate Mint Brownies … fluffy filling & frosted
Large Box of Brownie Mix

Filling:
2 c powdered sugar
½ c butter or margarine, softened
1 T water
½ t mint extract
3 drops green food coloring

Topping:
10 oz mint chocolate chips
9 T butter

Make brownies according to package directions and bake in a 13 x 9 x 2
inch pan. Bake at 350 degrees for 30 minutes. (Top of brownies will still
appear wet). Cool completely. Combine filling ingredients in a medium
mixing bowl; beat until creamy. Spread over cooled brownies. Refrigerate
until set. For topping, melt chocolate chips and butter over low heat in a
small saucepan. Let cool for 30 minutes or until lukewarm, stirring
occasionally. Spread over filling. Chill before cutting. Store in
refrigerator. Makes 5-6 dozen.

Microwave Brownies ... quick and easy

⅔ c margarine
1 c sugar
2 eggs, slightly beaten
1 t vanilla
1 c sifted flour

¼ c cocoa
¼ c instant cocoa mix
½ t baking powder
½ c chopped nuts

Melt margarine in bowl on high for one minute or until melted. Add sugar. Cool. Add eggs, and vanilla. Sift flour, dry cocoa, instant cocoa and baking powder into sugar mixture and blend in. Stir in nuts. Pour into lightly greased 9 inch baking dish. Cook on high in microwave for 4½ to 5½ minutes. Cool before cutting.

Blonde Brownies ... an oldie, but goodie

⅔ c oil
2 c brown sugar, packed
2 eggs
2 T water
½ c nuts

2 c flour
1 T salt
¼ t baking soda
1 t baking powder
2 t vanilla
6 oz chocolate chips

Mix all ingredients except chocolate chips and spread in a 10 x 14 inch pan. Sprinkle chocolate chips on top and bake at 350 degrees for about 30 minutes or until done.

Chocolate Chip Cookie Bars ... often requested recipe

2 c finely crushed cornflakes
⅓ c butter or margarine, melted
2 T sugar
¼ c each milk chocolate, peanut butter, semisweet chocolate and vanilla or white chips(or any combination)

1 c flaked coconut
1 c chopped favorite nuts
1 can (14 oz) sweetened condensed milk

In a bowl, combine the cornflake crumbs, butter and sugar. Press into a greased 13 x 9 x 2 inch baking pan. Sprinkle with chips, coconut and nuts. Drizzle with milk. Bake at 350 degrees for 25 minutes. Cool on a wire rack before cutting. Makes about 2 dozen.

Chocolate Chip Caramel Nut Bars ... Caramelicious

1 package (18-oz.) refrigerated chocolate chip cookie dough, softened, divided

½ cup chopped walnuts, divided
½ cup caramel ice cream topping

Preheat oven to 350° F. Grease 9-inch-square baking pan. Press ¾ package of cookie dough into prepared baking pan. Bake for 10 minutes. Sprinkle ¼ cup nuts over cookie crust; drizzle caramel topping over nuts. Top with teaspoonfuls of remaining cookie dough; press gently into caramel topping. Sprinkle with remaining nuts. Bake for 14 to 18 minutes or until edge is set. Cool in pan on wire rack.

Coffee and Spice Drops

1 c soft shortening
2 c brown sugar
2 eggs
½ c cold coffee.
3½ cups flour

1 t soda
1 t salt
1 t nutmeg
1 t cinnamon
raisins and nuts (optional)

Mix first three ingredients thoroughly, then stir in the cold coffee. Stir in remaining ingredients. Chill at least one hour if possible. Drop rounded teaspoonfuls about 2 inches apart on lightly greased baking sheet. Bake until set, when touched lightly with finger leaves no imprint. Cook at 400 degrees for 8-10 minutes. Makes 6 dozen

Chess Brownies ... yummy cheesecake brownies

1 Duncan Hines yellow cake mix
1 stick butter, softened
1 egg

2 eggs, well beaten
8 oz cream cheese
3 cup powdered sugar

Blend cake mix, butter and 1 egg. Press into a 9 x 13 inch baking dish with floured hands. Blend beaten eggs, cream cheese and sugar until smooth. Pour over pressed mixture and bake at 350 degrees for 35-40 minutes.

This is one of my most-requested recipes.

Chocolate Lemon Cream Bars

1 pkg devil's food cake mix
½ c butter or margarine, softened
1 egg
½ c chopped walnuts
Filling:
8 oz cream cheese, softened

14 oz can sweetened condensed
    milk
1 egg
3 T lemon juice
2-3 t grated lemon zest(peel)

In a large mixing bowl, beat the cake mix, butter and egg on low speed until combined. Stir in walnuts. Set aside 1 cup for topping. Press the remaining mixture into a greased 13 x 9 x 2 baking dish. Bake at 350 degrees for 8-10 minutes or until set. Cool for 5 minutes.

In a mixing bowl, beat cream cheese until smooth. Add milk, egg, lemon juice and peel; mix well. Pour over the crust. Crumble reserved cake mixture over the top. Bake for 18-22 minutes or until set. Cool completely before cutting. Store in the refrigerator. Makes 4 dozen.

Chocolate Brownies ... layers of love

¾ c all-purpose flour
¾ c cocoa
¼ t salt
½ c (1 stick) real butter cut in
    pieces
½ c granulated sugar
½ c packed brown sugar

3 large eggs, divided
2 t vanilla extract
1 c chopped pecans
¾ c white chips
½ c caramel ice cream topping
¾ c chocolate chips

Preheat oven to 350 degrees . Grease 8-inch-square baking pan. Combine cocoa, flour and salt in small bowl. Beat butter, granulated sugar and brown sugar in large mixer bowl until creamy. Add 2 eggs, one at a time, beating well after each addition. Add vanilla extract; mix well. Gradually beat in flour mixture. Reserve ¾ cup batter. Spread remaining batter into prepared baking pan. Sprinkle pecans and white morsels over batter. Drizzle caramel topping over top.

Beat remaining egg and reserved batter in same large bowl until light in color. Stir in semi-sweet morsels. Spread evenly over caramel topping.

Bake for 30 to 35 minutes or until center is set. Cool completely in pan on wire rack. Cut into squares.

White Chocolate Oatmeal Cookies

1 c butter, softened
½ c sugar
½ c packed brown sugar
1 egg
3 t vanilla
6 1-oz squares white baking
  chocolate, melted

1 t coconut extract
¼ c flour
1 t salt
1 t baking soda
1½ c quick cooking oats
1 c flaked coconut, toasted
  additional sugar

In mixing bowl, cream butter and sugars. Add egg and extracts and mix well. Stir in melted chocolate. Combine flour, salt and baking soda; gradually add to creamed mixture. Stir in the oats and coconut. Drop by tablespoon 3 inches apart onto an un-greased baking sheet. Flatten with a glass dipped in sugar. Bake at 350 degrees for 9 -11 minutes or until golden brown. Cool for 1 minute before removing to wire racks. Makes about 5 dozen.

Coconut Chews ... an oldie, but goodie

⅔ c margarine
1½ c brown sugar
1 c sifted flour
½ t salt
2 eggs

1 t baking powder
1 t vanilla
1 c coconut
¾ c nuts, more or less

Melt margarine in large pan; blend in sugar. Sift flour, salt and baking powder. Combine all ingredients with the brown sugar mixture. Bake in a greased and floured 11 x 7 inch pan for 25-30 minutes at 350 degrees.

Chocolate Krispies

3 c Rice Krispies
7 graham crackers, whole
2½ c miniature marshmallows
12 oz chocolate chips

⅔ c light corn syrup
3 T margarine or butter
½ c crunchy peanut butter

Spray 13 x 9 x 2 inch microwave pan with cooking spray. Place 6 whole graham crackers in single layer in bottom. Cut remaining piece to fit in bottom. Sprinkle marshmallows over crackers. Microwave on high 1 minute or until marshmallows are puffy. Cool.

In a 2 qt microwave safe bowl, combine chocolate chips, corn syrup and margarine. Microwave at high about 1 ½ minutes or until chocolate can be stirred smooth. Stir in peanut butter. Add Rice Krispies, mixing until combined. Spread evenly over marshmallows. Cover and refrigerate about 1 hour or until firm.

Cranberry Krispies … from a bread mix

15.6oz pkg cranberry quick
    bread mix
½ c melted margarine

½ c chopped walnuts or pecans
1 egg
½ c dried cranberries

Combine bread mix, butter, nuts, and egg; Stir in cranberries. Roll into 1-1/4 in balls. Place on un-greased cookie sheet. Flatten to 1/8 in thick with a glass dipped in sugar. Bake at 350 degrees for 10-12 minutes until lightly browned. Makes 2½ dozen.

Cream Cheese Krispies

½ c butter
3 oz cream cheese, softened
½ c sugar
¼ t almond extract
1 c flour

2 t baking powder
¼ t salt
1½ c Rice Krispies, crushed
red and green candied cherries

Cream together first four ingredients. Sift flour, baking powder and salt. Stir into butter mixture. Chill one or two hours, if time allows. Shape into balls and roll in the Rice Krispies crumbs. Place on un-greased cookie sheets; top each with a cherry and bake for 12-15 minutes at 350 degrees.

Death-by-Chocolate Cookies

2 8-oz pkg Baker's semi sweet
  chocolate, or summer coating
¾ c firmly packed brown sugar
¼ c margarine
2 eggs

1 t vanilla
½ c flour
¼ t baking powder
2 c chopped pecans

Heat oven to 350 degrees. Coarsely chop half of the chocolate (8 squares); set aside. Microware remaining 8 squares chocolate in large bowl on high 1-2 minutes. Do not overheat. Stir until chocolate is melted and smooth. Stir in sugar, butter, eggs and vanilla. Stir in flour and baking powder. Stir in reserved chopped chocolate and nuts. Drop by ¼ cupfuls onto an un-greased cookie sheet. Bake 12-13 minutes or until cookies rise and are set to the touch. Cool on cookie sheet for one minute. Transfer to waxed paper. Makes 15-20 cookies.

If you want bar cookies to be crisp on the bottom, use a metal pan, not a glass pan. Glass pans make bars soft on the bottom and they often stick.

Egg Kisses … an old and very good recipe

3 large egg whites
1 c sugar
¼ t cream of tartar

1 t vanilla
¾ c chocolate chips
½ c chopped nuts

Beat egg whites, vanilla, and cream of tartar in large glass bowl until foamy. Gradually add sugar and beat until stiff and glossy peaks are formed. Add chocolate chips and nuts. Drop by teaspoonful onto 2 cookie sheets lined with large brown paper bags. (Do not grease bags) Cook for 1 hour at 275 degrees. Turn off oven and don't open door until oven cools.

Works best if you let them sit in oven overnight. Egg Kisses are light and airy meringues, like no other cookie, I have ever eaten.

Cereal Snack Meringues

3 egg whites
⅔ c sugar

4 cups high fiber cereal flakes, like Total
½ c chocolate chips

Preheat oven to 325 degrees. Spray cookie sheet with nonstick cooking spray. In a medium bowl, beat egg whites and sugar together until glossy and stiff; fold in cereal and chocolate chips. Drop by tablespoonful onto cookie sheet 2 inches apart. Bake approximately 15 minutes or until golden brown. Allow to cool completely; store in airtight container. Makes 12-15 cookies.

Sugar-Free Strawberry Meringues

¼ c plus ½ c Splenda divided
1½ T cornstarch
3 large egg whites at room
temperature

¼ t cream of tartar
1½ t strawberry extract
few drops of red food coloring

In a small bowl, mix ¼ cup Splenda with cornstarch and set aside. In a medium bowl with an electric mixer on high speed, beat together egg whites and cream of tartar until soft peaks form. Gradually beat in remaining ½ cup of Splenda. Reduce mixer to medium speed and gradually add Splenda and cornstarch mixture until well-incorporated. Add strawberry extract and food coloring, increase speed to high, and beat until stiff and glossy peaks form, about 3 to 5 minutes. Drop by heaping teaspoonfuls onto baking sheets lined with parchment paper. Bake in a preheated 225 degrees oven until firm to the touch and crisp, approximately 1½ hours. Cool meringues thoroughly and store in an airtight container. Makes 4 dozen.
Variation, a cappuccino meringue: add 1 ½ teaspoon instant coffee in place of strawberry extract and food coloring

Graham Cracker Cookies

Melt and boil for 3 minutes:
1 c margarine
1 c brown sugar
½ t cinnamon

Pour sugar mixture over:
2 pkgs separated graham
crackers on a deep-lipped
cookie sheet.

Sprinkle with 2 cups chopped nuts and bake for 10 minutes at 400 degrees. Remove immediately and put onto waxed paper.

Kate's Hello Dolly Cookies

Melt 2 T margarine in a 9 x 11 in pan, then sprinkle the following in layers:

1½ c graham cracker crumbs (roll about 18 crackers yourself;
 the packaged kind doesn't work as well here)
1 c angel flake coconut
1 c chocolate chips
1 c butterscotch chips
1 c chopped nuts

Pour one can of sweetened condensed milk over the top, evenly. Bake at 350 degrees for 20-30 minutes, and then cool thoroughly before cutting into squares.

This is one of our family's favorite cookies.

Coconut Cranberry Bars … a treasured recipe

1½ c graham cracker crumbs(24 crackers)
½ c butter or margarine melted
1½ c vanilla or white chips

1½ c dried cranberries
14oz can sweetened condensed milk
1 c flaked coconut
1 c pecan halves

Combine cracker crumbs and butter; press into a greased 13 x 9 x 2 inch baking dish. In a bowl, combine the remaining ingredients; mix well. Gently spread over the crust. Bake at 350 degrees for 25-28 minutes or until edges are golden brown. Cool pan on wire rack. Cut into bars. Makes 3 dozen.

Lemon Angel Bars … easy, yummy bars

1-lb box, one-step Angel Food Cake Mix
21-oz can prepared lemon pie filling

Preheat oven to 350 degrees. Mix the two ingredients together and pour into an un-greased 10½ x 15½ inch jellyroll pan. Bake for 20 to 25 minutes. Cool and cut into 24 squares.

Knock-Your-Socks-Off Brownies

1 pkg German chocolate cake mix   ½ c melted butter
1 c chopped nuts   14 oz pkg vanilla caramels (40)
⅓ c + ½ c evaporated milk, divided   1 c chocolate chips

In a large mixing bowl, combine dry cake mix, nuts, ⅓ cup evaporated milk and melted butter. Press half of the batter into the bottom of a greased 13 x 9 inch glass-baking dish. Bake in a preheated 350-degree oven for 8 minutes.

In the microwave melt caramels with remaining ½ cup evaporated milk. When caramel mixture is well mixed, pour over baked layer. Cover with chocolate chips. Chill for about an hour or until the caramel is hard. Press the remaining batter on top of morsels. Return to oven and bake 28 minutes (or less for gooier brownies). Cool before cutting.

Chocolate Graham Cracker Treats

¾ c graham cracker crumbs (about   2 c powdered sugar
   12 squares), crushed   ½ c chunky peanut butter
½ c butter or margarine, melted   1 c chocolate chips

In a bowl, combine cracker crumbs and butter; mix well. Stir in sugar and peanut butter. Press into a greased 8 inch square pan. In a microwave, melt the chocolate chips and stir until smooth…for a minute on 50% power several times until melted. Spread over peanut butter layer and chill. Store in refrigerator. Makes 2 dozen

Lemon Bars

Crust:
1 c flour
⅓ c softened margarine
¼ c powdered sugar

Topping:
1 c sugar
2 c flour
½ t lemon extract
½ t baking powder
2 eggs
2 T lemon juice
¼ t salt

Combine crust and pat into 8-inch square baking pan. Bake 375 for 15 minutes, meanwhile, combine sugar, eggs, flour, lemon juice, extract, baking powder, and salt in mixing bowl. Mix until frothy. Pour over crust. Bake 375 degrees for 18-22 minutes or until golden brown. Dust with powdered sugar.

Grandma's No-Bake Chocolate Cookies

Mix and boil for 2 minutes:
2 c sugar
⅓ c cocoa
½ t vanilla

½ c milk
1 stick margarine

Remove from heat and add:
2½ c uncooked oatmeal
4 T peanut butter

Mix together. May also add ½ cup raisins. Drop by teaspoonful onto waxed paper. Cool.

Cookie or candy? Very quick and very good.

There are two things you give your children,
One is roots, the other is wings.
—Unknown

The Turkey Story

For many years my family gathered at my Grandmother Dickinson's home at 321 W. Washington Street in Glasgow, Kentucky, for Thanksgiving dinner. After her death we continued to meet there, where my Uncle Lewis and Aunt Selma then lived. In recent years the gathering has moved to the church where space allows the assembly of more than a hundred aunts, uncles, grandparents and cousins, nieces and nephews.

My grandmother, a widow of many years, was a model of fortitude and Southern gentility. This story of one of her early 1950s Thanksgiving dinners has become family lore —

Imagine a perfectly ironed white table cloth on a monstrous table, a high ceiling from which is suspended an elaborate cut-glass chandelier, 20 gleaming white plates each sitting before a high-backed chair standing at regal attention, napkins and expensive silverware perfectly arranged, and crystal goblets reflecting the light of candles. And in the vestibule a separate table waiting for the children.

Presently, the entire assembly is seated around their respective tables, the Dickinson prayer has been offered, each goblet is filled with the sweet nectar of iced tea, and the two servants begin to bring in dish after steaming dish from the kitchen, bowls heaping with mountains of mashed potatoes and green beans, numerous casseroles of delectable vegetables in all denominations, hot rolls redolent of yeast and fresh butter, and finally the culmination of hours of preparation—the gigantic turkey—unequaled in size and quality and roasted to a golden brown. But before Lizzie can set the tremendous foul before the host for carving, it slips from the platter to thud jarringly on the hardwood floor where it lies motionless, like the dead bird it is. The room comes to an utter and awkward silence.

At this point, my grandmother, with her legendary calmness in the face of such tragedy, gently says, "That's all right, Lizzie. Take it back to the kitchen and bring out the *other* turkey."

Macadamia Nut Cookies ... yummeee

1 c butter or margarine, softened
¾ c sugar
¾ c packed brown sugar
2 eggs
2¼ c flour
1 t vanilla

1 t baking soda
1 t salt
2 jars (3.5 oz each) macadamia
    nuts, chopped
2 c chocolate chips
1 c vanilla or white chips

In mixing bowl, cream butter and sugars, add eggs and vanilla. Beat on medium speed for two minutes, combine flour, baking soda and salt. Add to creamed mixture and beat for two minutes. Stir in chips and nuts, cover and refrigerate for several hours, if time allows. Drop by tablespoons, two inches apart on un-greased baking sheets. Bake at 350 degrees for 10-12 minutes or until golden brown. Cool on pans for one minute before removing to wire racks. Makes about 6 dozen.

Macaroon Bars

3¼ c flaked coconut, divided
14 oz sweetened condensed milk

1 t almond extract
1 tube refrigerated crescent rolls

Sprinkle 1 ½ cups coconut into a well-greased 13 x 9 x 2 inch pan. Combine milk and almond extract: drizzle half over the coconut. Unroll crescent dough; arrange in a single layer over coconut. Drizzle with remaining milk mixture; sprinkle with remaining coconut. Bake at 350 degrees for 30-35 minutes or until golden brown. Cool completely before cutting. Store in the refrigerator. Makes 3 dozen.

Meltaways

1 pkg. Devil's Food Cake
¼ c water
¼ c brown sugar, packed

½ c chopped nuts
1 pkg creamy white frosting tub
3 oz chocolate chips

Preheat oven to 375 degrees. Combine half the cake mix, the water, eggs, butter, brown sugar in the mixing bowl. Mix thoroughly. Blend in remaining cake mix. Stir in nuts. Spread in greased and floured jelly roll pan (15 ½ x 10 ½) Bake 20-25 minutes. Cool

Spread frosting on cake. Melt chocolate chips in microwave on 50% power and spread over frosting. Chill and cut when chocolate is completely firm.

Molasses Cookies ... old fashioned and spicy

½ c butter, softened
½ c shortening
1½ c sugar
½ c molasses
2 eggs, lightly beaten
4 c flour

½ t salt
2¼ t baking soda
2¼ t ground ginger
1½ t ground cloves
1½ t cinnamon
additional sugar

In a large mixing bowl, cream butter, shortening and sugar until light colored and fluffy. Beat in molasses and eggs.

In another large bowl, combine flour, salt, baking soda, ginger, cloves and cinnamon. Mix thoroughly. Gradually mix flour mixture into butter mixture until dough is blended and smooth.

Chill dough for about 10 minutes. Roll dough into 1½ inch balls; dip one side into sugar. Place cookies 2½ inches apart on a greased cookie sheet. Bake at 350 degrees for about 11 minutes. Do not over bake. Remove from cookie sheet and place on wire racks to cool. Makes about 3 dozen. Store in tightly covered container to keep soft. If they become too crisp, put a small slice of an apple in container to help soften.

Mint Sandwich Cookies

1 can vanilla frosting
½ t peppermint extract
3-5 drops green food coloring,
    optional

72 Ritz crackers
1 lb dark chocolate candy coating,
    or summer coating, coarsely
    chopped

In a bowl, combine the frosting, extract and food coloring if desired. Spread over half of the crackers; top with remaining crackers. Place candy coating in a microwave-safe bowl. Microwave on high for 1 ½ minutes or until smooth. Stir until all chocolate is melted. Dip the cookies in coating. Place on waxed paper until chocolate is completely set. Store in a airtight container at room temperature. Makes 3 dozen.

> Give a man a fish and he has food for a day; teach him how to fish
> and you can get rid of him for the entire weekend.
> — Zenna Schaffer

99

Oatmeal Cookies ... best oatmeal cookie ever

1 c shortening	2 t baking powder
2 c brown sugar, packed	1 T cinnamon
2 eggs	½ c chopped nuts
1 T vinegar	½ c raisins
1½ c flour	2 c oatmeal
⅓ t salt	

Cream shortening and sugar. Add vinegar, add eggs, and beat well after each addition. Add flour sifted, salt, baking powder and cinnamon. Add raisins, nuts and oatmeal. Bake for 10 minutes at 375 degrees.

Vinegar is the secret to these delicious cookies. You can add a cup of chocolate chips to this recipe to make it even better.

Oatmeal Cookies ... another winner

1 c butter or margarine, melted	pinch of salt
2 eggs	1¼ c of flour
1 c white sugar	½ c pecans
1 box vanilla instant pudding	1 c raisins
¾ c firmly packed brown sugar	1 t vanilla
1 t soda	3½ c quick cook oats

Cream butter, sugar, soda, salt, and egg. Add vanilla, flour, raisins, pudding and nuts until smooth. Add oats last. Drop from spoon onto un-greased baking sheet about 2 inches apart. Bake at 375 degrees for 9 minutes.

Peanut Butter Blossoms ... from Bisquick

½ c peanut butter	2 c Bisquick
1 can sweetened condensed milk	Hershey Chocolate Kisses

Combine all ingredients except the kisses and roll into balls. Flatten and place on a greased cookie sheet. Bake at 350 degrees for 10-12 minutes. While warm, place an unwrapped Hershey's kiss on top.

Oatmeal Rice Krispies Cookies... school cafeteria's

1 c sugar
1 c brown sugar, packed
1 c oil
1 c soft butter
1 egg
1 t salt
1 t baking soda
1 t vanilla

3½ c flour
1 c Rice Krispies
1 c quick oats, uncooked
½ c coconut

Optional:
1 c chopped nuts
1 c chocolate chips

Preheat oven to 350 degrees. In a large bowl, mix sugars, oil, egg and butter until evenly blended. Stir in baking soda, salt and flour. Mix well. Add vanilla, Rice Krispies, coconut and oats. Stir again, until dough is even. Drop by teaspoonfuls on an un-greased baking sheet. Bake from 10 to 12 minutes, or until edges are golden. Makes about 3 dozen.

Pumpkin Oatmeal Cookies

2 c flour
1 c old-fashioned oats
1 t baking soda
1 t cinnamon
1 c margarine, softened
1 c firmly packed brown sugar

1 c sugar
1 egg, slightly beaten
1 t vanilla
1 c solid packed pumpkin
1 c chocolate chips

Combine flour, oats, baking soda and cinnamon. In a separate bowl, cream butter and gradually add sugars beating until fluffy. Add egg, vanilla and pumpkin, mix well.

Gradually, add dry ingredients with pumpkin mixture. Add chocolate chips and stir by hand. Drop by teaspoonfuls onto cookie sheets and press slightly. Bake for 20 minutes at 350 degrees or until firm and lightly browned.

Orange Crispy Cookies ... cookies from a cake mix

1 pkg white cake mix
½ c butter or margarine, melted
1 egg, beaten
2 t grated orange peel

2 t orange extract
1 c rice crispy cereal
1 c chopped walnuts, optional

In a mixing bowl, combine the first five ingredients; mix well. Stir in cereal and walnuts if desired. Roll into 1 inch balls. Place 2 inches apart on un-greased baking sheets. Bake at 350 degrees for 12-14 minutes or until lightly browned. Cool for 1 minute before removing to wire racks. Makes about 4 dozen.

Orange Slice Cookies ... candy in a cookie

1 small pkg yellow cake mix, like
    Jiffy Cake Mix
1 large egg

3 T oil
1 c chopped pecans
10 orange slice candies, chopped

Preheat oven to 350 degrees. Stir together all ingredients until blended. Drop by tablespoon unto un-greased baking sheets. Bake for 8-10 minutes or until edges begin to brown. Remove and place on wire racks to cool. Makes 2 dozen.

Pecan Sandies ... favorite, old time wedding cookie

1 c butter
⅓ c sugar
2 t water

1 t vanilla
2 c flour (sifted)
1 c chopped pecans

Mix butter and sugar. Add water and vanilla and mix well. Add flour and pecans. Chill if time permits. Shape into walnut sized balls and bake on an un-greased cookie sheet at 325 degrees for 20 minutes. Cool slightly and roll in powdered sugar.

This is a favorite old-time recipe. Magee's Bakery in Lexington makes a similar cookie, but flattens it, and instead of rolling it in the powdered sugar, places a dollop of colored powder sugar icing on top when it is baked.

Peanut Butter Blossoms … classic goodie

½ c smooth peanut butter
½ c vegetable shortening
½ c sugar
½ c brown sugar
1 egg
1 t vanilla

2 T milk
1¾ cup flour
1 t baking soda
1 t salt
extra sugar
48 Hershey's kisses, unwrapped

In a large mixing bowl, combine the peanut butter, shortening and sugars. Beat at medium speed until well blended. Beat in the egg, milk, and vanilla. In a separate bowl, mix the flour, baking soda, and salt together.

Shape dough into 1" round balls. Roll each ball in granulated sugar to coat lightly. Place on un-greased baking sheets, about 2" apart. Bake at 375° for 10 to 12 minutes, or until very lightly browned.

Allow to cool on cookie sheets for about a minute then transfer to a waxed paper. Immediately, while cookies are still very warm, place a Hershey kiss in the center of each one, pressing gently into the cookie. Cool completely and allow the Hershey's kisses to harden before storing the cookies. This may take several hours

Double Peanut Butter Cookies

18-oz tube refrigerated sugar
   cookie dough
⅓ c peanut butter, smooth or
   crunchy

⅓ c flour
½ c coarsely chopped roasted
   peanuts
½ t vanilla

Preheat oven to 350 degrees. In a mixing bowl, use your hands to break up the cookie dough. Add the flour, peanut butter, peanuts and vanilla. Use your hands to knead the dough until the ingredients are fully incorporated. Drop the dough by tablespoons onto a baking sheet, at least 1½ inches apart. Dip the times of a fork into flour, then press the cookies twice, in a crisscross design, to flatten them to about ½ inch thickness.

Bake until the cookies are golden and the edges are lightly browned, 12 to 14 minutes. Use a spatula to transfer the cookies to a rack to cool completely. Makes about 40 cookies.

Peanut Butter 'n' Fudge Bars ... a real winner

2 c firmly packed brown sugar
1 c butter, softened
¼ c plus 2 T peanut butter, divided
2 eggs
2 c flour
1 t baking soda

¼ t salt, optional
2 c Quaker oats
14-oz can sweetened condensed milk
12 oz chocolate chips
⅔ c chopped peanuts

Heat oven to 350 degrees. Grease 13 x 9 inch baking pan. In large mixing bowl, beat brown sugar, butter and ¼ c peanut butter until light and fully. Beat in eggs. Add combined four, baking soda and salt; beat until well mixed. Stir in oats; mix well. Reserve 1 c of oat mixture; set aside. Spread remaining oat mixture evenly. In a small saucepan, combine milk, chocolate chips, and remaining 2 T peanut butter. Cook over low heat until chocolate is melted, stirring constantly. Remove from heat; stir in peanuts. Spread mixture evenly over crust in pan. Drop remaining oat mixture by teaspoonfuls evenly over chocolate mixture. Bake 25 to 30 minutes or until light golden brown. Cool completely on wire. Cut into bars. Makes 32 bars.

P B & J Bars ... delicious treats for big and little kids

1 pkg (18 oz) refrigerated sugar
    cookie dough, divided
⅔ c strawberry jam

¾ c granola cereal with raisins
¾ c peanut butter chips

Line a 9 inch square baking pan with foil and grease the foil. Press two-thirds of the cookie dough into prepared pan. Spread jam over dough to within ¼ inch of edge. In a mixing bowl, beat the granola, peanut butter chips and remaining dough until blended. Crumble over jam. Bake in a 350 degree oven for 20 minutes or until browned.

Peanut Butter Fingers ... one of the best!

1 c butter
1 c white sugar
1 c brown sugar   *Topping:*
2 eggs   12 oz chocolate chips
⅔ c peanut butter   ½ c powdered sugar
1 t baking soda   ¼ c peanut butter
½ t salt   2 T milk
1 t vanilla
2 c flour
2 c oatmeal

Preheat oven to 350 degrees Cream together butter and sugars. Add eggs
and peanut butter. Stir until smooth. Add remaining ingredients (excluding
topping ingredients) and mix until evenly blended. Grease a
9 x 13 inch baking dish. Press mixture evenly into pan. Bake for 25
minutes.

Remove from oven, cover immediately with chocolate chips and allow chips
to melt, then spread evenly.   Blend together powdered sugar, peanut butter
and milk until smooth. Spread topping mixture evenly over the melted
chocolate chips, making a swirl pattern. Cool, cut and serve.

Peanut Chocolate Cookies

1 c chunky peanut butter   ½ c water
2 T oil   12 oz milk chocolate candy bars,
2 eggs   coarsely chopped
1 pkg fudge brownie mix for   ½ c unsalted peanuts
   13 x 9 inch pan

In a large mixing bowl, cream peanut butter and oil. Beat in eggs just until
combined. Stir in brownie mix and water. Fold in the chopped candy bars
and peanuts. Drop by heaping tablespoons 2 inches apart onto greased
baking sheets. Bake for 350 degrees for 12-14 minutes or until lightly
browned. Remove to wire racks to cool. Makes 3½ dozen.

Cooking Rule... If at first you don't succeed, order pizza.
—Anonymous

Pecan Pie Bars ... thin, golden and yummy

8 oz refrigerated crescent rolls   ½ c corn syrup
1 egg   1 T butter or margarine, melted
½ c sugar   ½ t milk
½ c chopped pecans

Unroll crescent dough into a rectangle; press into the bottom and ½ inch up the sides of a greased 13 x 9 x 2 inch baking pan. Seal seams and perforations. Bake at 375 degree for 5 minutes.

Meanwhile, in a bowl, combine the remaining ingredients. Pour over the crust. Bake for 16-20 minutes or until golden brown and bubbly. Cool completely before cutting. Makes 24.

Pineapple Cookies

1 c packed brown sugar   1 t baking powder
1 c white sugar   1 t soda
1 c shortening   1 t salt
2 eggs, beaten
1 T vanilla   *Icing:*
20-oz can crushed pineapple,   1 stick of butter
   drained, reserve syrup   powdered sugar(about 1 box)
4 c flour   ¼ c milk
                                                        2-3 T reserved pineapple syrup

Cream sugars with shortening. Add beaten eggs and vanilla and mix. Fold in drained pineapple. Combine all dry ingredients and add to pineapple mixture. Mix and drop onto baking sheet and bake 15 minutes at 375 degrees.

Icing: Melt butter on medium heat in a pan. Add powdered sugar until a thick mixture is formed. Add milk and reserved pineapple syrup. Remove form the heat and use a hand mixer to heat until the mixture turns a white color as it cools. Ice the cookies and let icing set up before storing.

Pumpkin Bars

2 c flour
2 t baking powder
1 t baking soda
½ t salt
2 t cinnamon
4 eggs

15-oz can pumpkin
1⅔ c sugar
1 c oil
1 c chopped pecans
1 recipe cream cheese frosting, below

Combine flour, baking powder, soda, salt and cinnamon; set aside. In a mixing bowl, beat together eggs, pumpkin, sugar and oil. Add flour mixture; beat well. Stir in pecans. Spread in an un-greased 15 x 10 baking dish. Bake in 350-degree oven for 25-30 minutes. Cool on wire rack, then frost with icing below and sprinkle chopped pecans on top. Cut into 24 bars.

Cream Cheese Icing:
3-oz pkg cream cheese, softened
¼ c margarine

1 t vanilla
2 c powdered sugar

In a bowl, beat together softened cream cheese, margarine and vanilla until fluffy. Gradually add powdered sugar, beating until smooth.

Peanut Butterscotches

2⅓ c flour
1 c shortening
1 c sugar
½ c brown sugar
1 c peanuts
1 t soda

1 pkg butterscotch morsels
1 t salt
2 eggs
1 t vanilla
⅔ c raisins

Sift flour, baking soda, and salt. Cream shortening, add sugar gradually and cream until fluffy. Add eggs and vanilla and mix well. Add sifted dry ingredients and mix well. Add peanuts, raisins and butterscotch morsels. Drop by spoonfuls on greased cookie sheets. Cook for 15 minutes at 350 degrees.

Pecan Tassies ... lots of work, but good

Crust:
3 oz Philadelphia cream cheese
½ c butter
1 c flour

Filling:
1 egg
¾ c brown sugar
1 T soft butter
1 t vanilla
⅛ t salt
⅔ c finely chopped pecans

Cream together the crust; divide into 24 balls and press into little muffin tins (little tiny cupcake pans)

Mix together the filling and fill the uncooked crust until ½ full. Bake at 350 degrees for 30 minutes.

Rob Roy Cookies ... spicy, nutty oatmeal cookie

1 c shortening
1½ c packed brown sugar
1 t salt
½ t cinnamon
½ t cloves
¼ c milk

2 eggs
1¾ c sifted flour
¾ t baking soda
1½ c each: rolled oats, English
    walnuts, raisins

Combine shortening, brown sugar, salt, spices, milk and eggs, beat thoroughly. Add flour and soda and stir until blended. Add nuts, oats, and raisins and mix thoroughly. Drop level tablespoon of dough on greased baking sheet. Flatten cookies with fork dipped in flour. Bake at 375 degrees for 10-20 minutes. 5 dozen

Raspberry Jam Bars

½ c butter or margarine
2 c white chocolate chips
2 large eggs
½ c sugar
1 c flour

½ t salt
½ t almond extract
½ c seedless raspberry jam
¼ cup toasted, sliced almonds

Preheat oven to 325 degrees. Grease and sugar a 9 inch square baking pan. Melt butter in microwave-safe bowl on High(100%) power for 1 minute; stir. Add 1 cup white chips; let stand. Do not stir. Beat eggs in large mixing bowl until foamy. Add sugar; beat until light lemon-colored, about 5 minutes. Stir in white chips mixture. Add flour, salt and almond extract; mix at low speed until combined. Spread ⅔ of batter into prepared pan.

Bake for 15-17 minutes or until light golden brown around edges. Remove from oven to wire rack.

Heat jam in small, microwave-safe bowl on HIGH(100%) power for 30 seconds; stir. Spread jam over warm crust. Stir remaining white chips into remaining batter. Drop spoonfuls of batter over jam. Sprinkle with almonds. Bake for 25-30 minutes or until edges are browned. Cool completely in pan on wire rack. Cut into bars.

Jeanne's Rum Brownies ... very easy and very good

1 brownie mix, with nuts or
    add ½ c nuts
2 cups powdered sugar
rum

1 t milk
1 t butter
6 oz chocolate chips

Make brownies according to directions on box. Cool. Add milk and butter to powdered sugar and enough rum to make easy to spread over brownies. Melt chocolate chips in microwave in a measuring cup on 50% power for 2 minutes. Stir until melted and drizzle in strings on top of rum icing.

Rocky Top Brownies

20-oz pkg fudge brownie mix
10-12 oz white baking pieces
1 c chocolate chip
½ c pecan pieces
¼ c butter, melted

3 T hot water
2 c sifted powdered sugar
¼ c cocoa
1 t vanilla
¾ c pecan pieces

Grease bottom of 13 x 9 x 2 inch baking dish. Set aside. Prepare brownie mix according to box directions . Stir in half of the white baking pieces, all of the chocolate chips, and ½ cup pecans. Spread the batter in the prepared baking pan.

Bake in a 350 degree oven for about 30 minutes or until center is set. Sprinkle with the remaining white baking pieces. Bake for 1 minute more. Cool in pan on a wire rack.

For frosting, in a small bowl combine melted butter and hot water; stir in powdered sugar, cocoa and vanilla. Beat by hand until smooth. Spoon over top of brownies. Sprinkle with the ¾ cup pecans. Cool about 1 ½ hours or until frosting is set . Cut into bars. Makes about 3 dozen.

Mary's Scotcheroos

Bring to a boil:
1 c sugar
1 c light corn syrup

Add:
6-7 c Rice Krispies
1 c peanut butter

Mix and spread in a buttered 9 x 13 inch pan.

Melt and spread over top:
6 oz chocolate chips
6 oz butterscotch chips

Pecan Pie Bars

3 large eggs

Crust:
1½ c flour
1 stick butter, softened
¼ c packed brown sugar

Filling:
¾ c corn syrup
¾ c sugar
2 T butter, melted
1 t vanilla
11½ oz chocolate chips
1½ c chopped pecans

Crust:
Beat flour, butter and brown sugar in small mixing bowl until crumbly. Press into a greased 13 x 9 Pyrex pan. In an oven preheated to 350 degrees, bake for 12-15 minutes or until lightly browned.

Filling:
Beat eggs, corn syrup, sugar, butter and vanilla in medium bowl with wire whisk. Stir in chips and nuts. Pour evenly over baked crust. Bake for 25-30 minutes or until set. Cool in the pan on a wire rack.

Scotch Bars ... good with butterscotch chips

2 c flour
2 t baking powder
1 t baking soda
1 t salt
1 c butter or margarine, softened

¾ c sugar
¾ c brown sugar, packed
2 eggs
1½ c uncooked quick oats
½ c nuts
11 oz butterscotch chips, divided

Preheat oven to 350 degrees. Grease a 9 x 13 inch pan. Combine flour, baking powder, baking soda and salt in a bowl and set aside. In a large mixing bowl, combine butter or margarine, sugars and eggs. Beat until creamy. Gradually blend in the flour mixture, oats, nuts, and 1 ½ cups of butterscotch chips. Pour into prepared pan: sprinkle with remaining chips. Bake at 350 degrees for 30-35 minutes, or until golden brown. Cool, cut into bars.

If cookies get hard in a cookie jar, don't toss them out; a piece of bread in the container will soften them almost immediately

Skillet Cookies

1 stick butter
1 c sugar
1 c chopped dates
2 eggs, beaten

1 c chopped pecans
3 c Rice Krispies
1½ t vanilla
powdered sugar

Melt margarine in heavy skillet. Add sugar, dates and beaten eggs. Cook over medium heat for 12 minutes, stirring constantly. Remove from heat and add pecans, cereal and vanilla. Cool and roll into balls and roll in powdered sugar.

Snickerdoodles ... a favorite crispy cookie

½ c margarine
½ c shortening
2½ c sugar
2 eggs

2½ c flour
1 t soda
2 t cream of tartar
1½ t salt

Cream margarine, shortening and sugar. Add eggs and blend. Sift dry ingredients and add to creamed mixture. Chill, if time permits, and shape into walnut sized balls. Roll in colored Christmas sugars or a sugar and cinnamon mixture. Place 2" apart on an un-greased cookie sheet and bake at 350 degrees for 16 minutes. Makes 4 dozen.

This crisp and chewy cookie has replaced Christmas Sugar Cookies at our house and is much easier to prepare. We always double this recipe.

Susan's Oatmeal Caramel Bars

Bars:
2 c flour
2 c quick-cooking rolled oats
1½ c firmly packed brown sugar
1 t baking soda
1¼ c margarine or butter, softened
½ t salt

Filling:
3 T flour
½ c nuts
6 oz chocolate chips
12½-oz jar caramel ice cream topping

Heat oven to 350 degrees. Grease 13 x 9 pan. In large bowl, combine all bar ingredients; mix at low speed until crumbly. Reserve half of crumb mixture (about 3 cups) for topping. Press remaining crumb mixture in bottom of greased pan. Bake at 350 degrees for 10 minutes. In a small bowl, combine caramel topping and 3 T of flour. Remove partially baked bars from oven; sprinkle with chocolate chips and nuts. Drizzle evenly with caramel mixture; sprinkle with reserved crumb mixture. Bake at 350 degrees for an additional 18-22 minutes or until golden brown. Cool. May refrigerate to set filling.

Brownie S'Mores

1 large pkg (19-21 oz) brownie mix
3 eggs
2 cups little marshmallows

6 T butter
¼ cup milk
12 whole graham crackers

Prepare brownie mix according to directions and bake in a 325-degree oven until done, about 25 minutes. A toothpick should come out fairly clean from the middle. Sprinkle the marshmallows on the top of the brownies and cover with the graham crackers as soon as they come out of the oven. Bake for 2 more minutes and remove the pan from the oven. Press the graham crackers down into the marshmallows. Cool on a wire rack and then turn out upside down. Invert and cut into graham cracker squares.

Laughter is brightest, in the place where the food is served.
- Irish Proverb

Pike County Reese's Pieces Cookies

1 pkg yellow cake mix
½ c peanut butter
¼ c soft butter

¼ c water
2 eggs
1 c Reese's pieces

Heat oven to 350 degrees. In large bowl combine cake mix, peanut butter, margarine or butter, water and eggs; stir until well blended. Fold in Reese's pieces. Drop by rounded teaspoonfuls 2 inches apart onto un-greased cookie sheets. Bake at 350 degrees for 8 to 12 minutes or until light golden brown. Immediately remove from cookie sheets. Makes 3½ dozen.

Ghosts ... Boo!

Nutter Butter cookies
white chocolate summer coating
Chocolate chips

Melt summer coating on lowest temperature in sauce pan. Watch carefully, to prevent burning. Dip cookies in chocolate and place on waxed paper. Add 2 chocolate chips for eyes and allow to dry.

Summer coating can be purchased in candy stores, and in large discount stores like Wal Mart. Comes in little patties.

Don't dig your grave with your own knife and fork.
— English Proverb

Cappuccino Brownies

Large brownie mix with nuts

For cream-cheese layer:
8 oz cream cheese, softened
¾ stick (6 T) unsalted
   butter, softened
1½ c confectioners' sugar
1 t vanilla extract
1 t ground cinnamon

For glaze:
6 oz good bittersweet chocolate
   (not unsweetened), finely chopped
2 T unsalted butter
½ c heavy cream
1½ T instant espresso powder,
   dissolved in 1 T boiling water

To make the brownie layer:
Put a rack in middle of oven and preheat oven to 350°F. Butter and flour a
13 x 9-inch baking pan, knocking off excess flour. Spread batter evenly in
baking pan. Bake until a wooden pick or skewer inserted in center comes
out with some crumbs adhering. Cook according to box directions. Cool
completely in pan on a rack.

To make the cream-cheese layer:
Beat together cream cheese and butter in a large bowl with an electric mixer
on medium speed until light and fluffy. Sift in confectioners' sugar, then add
vanilla and cinnamon, and beat until mixture is well-combined. Spread
cream cheese mixture evenly over cooled brownie layer. Refrigerate until
firm, about 1 hour.

To make the glaze:
Combine all ingredients in a pan set on stove on lowest heat, stirring, until
chocolate and butter are melted and glaze is smooth. Remove from heat and
cool to room temperature, stirring occasionally, about 20 minutes. Pour
glaze over cream-cheese layer, then spread evenly. Refrigerate brownies,
covered, until cold, about 3 hours. Cut into 40 bars.

Drinks

Iced Almond Tea ... fantastic

2 tea bags
2 c boiling water
2/3 c sugar or sweetener

4 T lemon juice
½ t almond extract
½ t vanilla
2 c ice-cold water

In a pot, add sugar, lemon juice and tea bags. Pour boiling water over tea mixture. Cover; let steep about 10 minutes. Remove tea bags. Add remaining ingredients. Cool to room temperature; then refrigerate until completely chilled. Serve over ice. Serves 4.

Oprah Winfrey is very fond of this summer treat ! I love it and keep a jar in the refrigerator that is made with sweetener and drink it instead of cola..

Rich Old Fashioned Hot Cocoa

¼ c sugar
¼ c cocoa powder
¼ t cinnamon
⅛ t salt
2 c milk

2 c half and half
1 t vanilla
Kool Whip
Orange zest (optional)

Mix cocoa, salt, cinnamon, and sugar in a 2 qt saucepan. Add 1 cup of the milk and stir to form a smooth paste. Gradually stir in the remaining 1 cup of milk. Place over low heat and warm to dissolve sugar and blend ingredients. Add half and half and vanilla extract. Heat until fine wisps of steam are rising from the surface of the hot cocoa. Pour into a warmed heavy mug. Garnish with whipped cream, a dusting of cinnamon, and orange zest, if desired.

Easy Cocoa Mix

2-lb box Nestlé's Quik
16-oz jar Coffee-mate

1-lb box powdered sugar
8-oz box dry milk

Mix all ingredients together well. Store in an airtight container. Use 3-4 heaping tablespoons of mix per cup of boiling water. Top with Kool Whip.

In the cookies of life, friends are the chocolate chips.

Cranberry Punch

1 qt cranberry juice cocktail
1 qt pineapple juice
¼ c sugar

2 t almond extract
2 liters (or qts) ginger ale, chilled

Combine first four ingredients, stirring until sugar dissolves. Cover and chill at least four hours. To serve, pour juice mixture into punch bowl and stir in ginger ale.

Lucy's Boiled Drinking Custard

1 half-gallon whole milk
6 eggs

¾ to 1 c sugar
vanilla

Heat milk until it gets a skim on top. Beat eggs with mixer. Add sugar and beat well. Add some hot milk to egg mixture. Add mixture to heated milk gradually, stirring constantly. Cook until custard thickens and coats a metal spoon. Stir mixture continuously. Remove from heat. *Optional*: Strain custard through gauze cloth. Add vanilla, 1½ teaspoon or to taste. Refrigerate and serve with dollop of whipped cream and sprinkle of nutmeg.

This old recipe is still great and is best when made the day before serving.

Bourbon Slush ... the St. Louie way

2 6-oz orange juice
2 6-oz lemonade
2 c Bourbon

9 c water
1 T instant tea
1¾ c sugar

Freeze in a plastic container. Mix frozen slush half and half with 7-up or favorite clear soda to serve.

Bourbon Slush ... Liz's Party Pleaser

2 tea bags
1 c boiling water
1 c sugar
3½ cups of cold water

6-oz can of orange juice, thawed
½ c bourbon
6 oz frozen lemonade, thawed
2 6-oz cans frozen limeade

Mix tea and boiling water and seep for 3-4 minutes. Stir in sugar. Stir in rest. Freeze until firm. Thaw until it "slushes." Serve "as is."

Vodka Slush ... makes 2 batches

2 6-oz cans frozen lemonade
1 6-oz can frozen orange juice
2 6-oz cans frozen limeade

Thaw the frozen juices, but not completely, and stir in 3½ cans of water

Add 1cup sugar (or more if your taste requires) and 2 cups of vodka, mix and freeze for at least 24 hours. When you serve, fill cup approximately ¾ full of your brew and top off with 7-up or Sprite.

Grape Wine

40 oz Welch's grape juice
4½ c sugar
½ t dry yeast

1-gallon jug
1 large balloon (10 c size)
1 qt water

Pour grape juice into a narrow neck jug. Mix sugar and yeast in saucepan and add 1 qt warm water to dissolve sugar. Pour into jug. Fill rest of jug with warm water and mix well. Stretch neck of balloon over top of jug. Set out of sunlight for 21 days. Balloon will gradually grow.

Remove balloon and drink ¼ of contents; find a soft spot to fall.

Orange Julius

1 c orange juice
1½ T sugar
½ c ice

½ c dry milk powder
½ t vanilla
1 scoop vanilla ice cream

Blend in blender until ice is crushed.

Labrot and Graham's Peach Tea

Dilute 1 quart of Tetley Peach Tea concentrate to 2 gallons with cold water. Serve "on the rocks."

This tea was served recently after a tour of the Labrot and Graham Distillery. It is really fantastic, and couldn't be easier. My husband said, "What kind of recipe is this?" I told him, "That,, my dear, is one even you can prepare."

"A good cook is like a sorceress who dispenses happiness."
— Elsa Schiapirel

Aunt Selma's Tea Punch ... a family & church favorite

2 c boiling water
1 c sugar
7 tea bags

12 oz frozen orange juice
12 oz frozen lemonade
water to make 1 gallon

Steep tea bags in hot water for 5 minutes. Add sugar and the rest of ingredients.

Diane's Wedding Punch

4 c sugar
6 c water
46 oz pineapple juice

12 oz frozen lemonade
12 oz frozen orange juice
6 bananas

Combine all ingredients; puree bananas in blender with small amount of juice. Mix all together and pour into 2-3 gallon size freezer bag and freeze over night. Place a frozen bag of punch into bowl and pour 2 liters of ginger ale over slush.

My wife and I go out to dinner and a movie every week . . .
She goes on Tuesdays and I go on Fridays.
— Tom and Ray Magliozzi (aka National
Public Radio's *Click and Clack—
The Tappet Brothers)*

Candies

Black Walnut Candy ... a very old family recipe

2 c brown sugar
1½ c black walnuts
1 lump butter

1 c milk
1 t Karo syrup (optional)

Put sugar, milk and karo on to cook and stir every now and then to keep from curdling. As soon as it starts to boil, add butter. When a few drops of the candy forms a soft ball in cold water, remove from fire and add walnuts. Let cool before beating. When thick and creamy, drop by spoonfuls on buttered dish or waxed paper.

Black Walnut Fudge

1 c black walnuts
2 c sugar
½ c cocoa

12 oz can evaporated milk
2 T butter
1 t vanilla

Mix walnuts, sugar and cocoa together in a saucepan. Add evaporated milk and bring to a boil. Cook, stirring constantly, until mixture forms a soft ball when dropped in cold water. Remove from heat; do not stir. Add butter and vanilla; let cool. Beat until creamy and pour into a buttered 8-inch square pan. Refrigerate.

Brown Sugar Fudge

¼ c margarine
1 c brown sugar
1 c white sugar

¾ c sour cream
1 t vanilla
½ c chopped walnuts

Melt butter in heavy saucepan. Add brown sugar and heat to boiling. Add sugar and sour cream. Cook over medium heat until sugar dissolves, then allow mixture to rise to a slightly higher heat of 236 degrees, without stirring. Cool at room temperature to lukewarm. Beat until mixture holds its shape and loses its gloss. Quickly add vanilla and nuts. Spread immediately in a buttered 8 in square pan. Makes about 50 pieces.

Columbus brought cacao (chocolate) beans back to Spain
from Panama on his fourth voyage in 1502.

Bourbon Fudge

2 c sugar
1 oz bitter chocolate
1 T corn syrup
1 rounded cup marshmallow cream
½ c evaporated milk
½ c chopped pecans

½ stick unsalted butter (not
   margarine)
5 T bourbon whiskey
6 oz semisweet chocolate chips
½ t vanilla

Line a 9 x 9 inch pan with aluminum foil. Butter the foil and set aside.
Cook sugar, syrup, evaporated milk and butter to 236 degrees, in a large
pot, stirring occasionally. Remove from heat. Add both the chocolates
and stir until melted. Add nuts and marshmallows. Mix. Add bourbon
and vanilla and mix. Pour into the pan. Cool to room temperature
uncovered. Cover with plastic and refrigerate until firm enough to cut.

*Candy is cooked to the soft-ball stage — when a few drops of the candy
dropped into cup of cold water can be formed into a soft ball, using your
fingers. Don't touch the candy while it's hot—it's very hot.*

LaVece's Bourbon Balls … from the Bluegrass

2 c chopped pecans
Bourbon to cover chopped nuts
2 boxes (at least) powdered sugar

1 stick margarine
1-2 lb *dark* chocolate summer coating

Soak chopped pecans in enough bourbon to cover. Soak as long as
possible, more than 24 hours of soaking makes better candy. Pour off
bourbon and save. Mix powdered sugar and margarine with enough of the
bourbon from the nuts to make a doughy mixture in a large bowl with an
electric mixer. Use more or less sugar and bourbon to make the right
consistency to work with your hands. Add the drained nuts and mix well.
(May need more sugar after adding nuts.) Roll into small balls and place on
waxed paper on cookie sheets. Carefully melt the summer coating a pound
at a time in a pan on the stove-top (lowest setting), stirring often. Caution—
too much heat will cause the summer coating to burn and clump. Hand dip
each piece with the thumb and middle finger. Shake off excess, roll off the
fingers and allow to dry on wax paper. Makes about 100 pieces.

*Summer coating lacks cocoa butter and is easily melted. It comes in all
kinds of flavors and may be purchased in many candy stores and in some
groceries. Most who try these bourbon balls tell me they are better than
Rebecca Ruth's. The real secret to this recipe though, is to "soak the nuts."*

Coconut Bonbons

2½ c dry coconut, finely shredded   ¾ c white Karo syrup
summer coating, your choice of flavors

Heat Karo syrup to just before it boils and mix in coconut. Let sit for a
while to cool. Firmly shape into about 50 balls. You may need to clean
your hands and wet them periodically. Dip in chocolate summer coating.

*I use green coating for coconut bonbons. My husband says to skip the
green or white stuff and go straight for the dark semi-sweet chocolate
coating which he says is far superior—the result is similar to a Mounds
candy bar.*

Christmas Fudge ... the old fashioned way

2 c sugar   ⅔ c milk
½ c cocoa   ¼ c white corn syrup
1 lump butter   1 t vanilla

Mix cocoa and sugar; add milk, corn syrup, and butter. Cook and stir until
it makes a firm ball when dropped in cold water. Cool and add vanilla and
beat well until it is firm enough to handle. Butter hands and gather it into a
large lump and knead well. Pinch off small pieces and roll into balls with
buttered hands. Decorate with pecan halves, candied cherries, chopped nuts
or coconuts.

"This is a good old time recipe and is always doubled at Christmas."

"Forget love... I'd rather fall in chocolate!"
— Unknown

Chocolate Covered Cherries

3 10-oz jars maraschino cherries
   with stems
3 T butter, softened
3 T corn syrup

2 c sifted powdered sugar
1 pound chocolate-flavored candy
   coating or summer coating

Drain cherries thoroughly on paper towel for several hours. Line a baking sheet with waxed paper; set baking sheet aside.

In a small mixing bowl combine butter and corn syrup. Stir in powdered sugar; knead mixture till smooth. (May need to add a little more powdered sugar to be able to handle). Shape about ½ teaspoon powdered sugar mixture around each cherry. Place coated cherries, stem side up, on the prepared baking sheet. Chill about an hour or till firm (Do not chill too long as the powder sugar will begin to dissolve.)

Melt candy coating in a pan on stove on lowest temperature. Stir to complete the melting process. Line a baking sheet with waxed paper. Holding cherries by the stem, dip the balls in the chocolate. Be sure to completely seal cherries to prevent cherries from leaking. Let excess chocolate drip off. Place cherries stem sides up on prepared baking sheet.

Chill till coating is firm. Store in a tightly covered container in the refrigerator. Let cherries stay in the refrigerator for 1 or 2 weeks to allow the acid of the cherries to cause the powdered sugar to liquefy. Makes 60.

Chocolate Cream Mints ... easy and yummy

3 oz cream cheese
2¼ c confectioner's sugar
chocolate summer coating

Combine cheese and sugar and pinch off pieces of the dough, roll into balls and roll in granulated sugar. (You can flavor the dough with any oil flavorings such as cherry, strawberry, lemon, peppermint, etc. but they are good plain, too). Place dough balls on wax paper on a cookie sheet or tray; flatten with fork and let dry.

These may be dipped in any flavor summer coating. Don't roll them in granulated sugar, though, if you plan to dip them in chocolate.

Cranberry Nut Fudge ... love this one at Christmas

1 t butter
16-oz can milk chocolate frosting
12 oz chocolate chips

6 oz dried cranberries
½ c chopped pecans

Line an 8-inch square dish with foil and grease the foil with butter; set aside. In a heavy saucepan, combine frosting and chocolate chips. Cook and stir over medium low heat until chips are melted. Stir in cranberries and nuts. Pour into prepared pan and refrigerate until firm, about 2 hours.

Using foil, lift fudge out of pan. Discard foil; cut the fudge into 1 inch squares. Store in refrigerator. Makes about 2 pounds.

Cranberry White Chocolate Clusters

12-oz pkg white chocolate chips or
    morsels
6-oz pkg sweetened dried
    cranberries

½ c chopped walnuts or pecans
½ c shredded coconut, optional

Line a cookie sheet with aluminum foil; set aside. Place chocolate in a microwave bowl. Microwave on medium-high (70 percent) power for a minute, stopping it to stir. Microwave in 10 to 20 second intervals, removing and stirring until chocolate is completely melted. Add remaining ingredients. Stir until thoroughly combined.

Drop by rounded teaspoonfuls onto cookie sheet. Let harden at room temperature. Store in a tightly sealed container. May store in refrigerator for 2 weeks. Makes 16 candies.

Principles have no real force, except when one is well fed.
— Mark Twain

129

Date-Nut Loaf ... an old, family treasure

2 c white sugar
1 c sweet milk
1 T butter

1 box dates, chopped
1 c chopped nuts

Boil sugar and milk, stirring occasionally until softball stage. Then add
dates and boil 5 minutes longer. Add nuts and butter and boil a few
minutes longer. Place pan in cold water to cool. When cool, beat with
spoon until firm enough to handle. Roll on marble top or waxed paper or
other smooth surface into two long narrow rolls. Wrap rolls in waxed paper
and put in cool place. After several hours or until used, slice into rounds.

Dad Hughes's Date-Nut Fudge

3 cups sugar
⅛ t salt
1 t vanilla
½ cup chopped nuts

1½ cup milk
¼ cup butter
1 box dates, chopped

Boil everything except butter until the soft boil stage. Add butter, beat
until candy begins to lose it's gloss, and is ready to spread. Add dates and
nuts. Pour into butter dish and cool.

Eggnog Fudge

2 t butter or margarine
2 c sugar
1 c eggnog
2 T corn syrup
2 T butter or margarine

1 t vanilla
½ c chopped walnuts or pecans
2 T chocolate chips

Butter sides of heavy 3 quart saucepan with 2 t butter. Cook sugar,
eggnog, and corn syrup over medium heat, stirring constantly, until sugar
dissolves and mixture comes to a boil. Cook to a soft-ball stage (238
degrees, stirring only as necessary. Immediately remove from heat and
cool to lukewarm (110°) without stirring. Add the 2 tablespoons of butter
or margarine and the vanilla. Beat vigorously until fudge becomes very
thick and starts to lose its gloss. Quickly stir in nuts. Spread in buttered
8x4x2-inch pan. Melt chocolate chips. Drizzle over top of fudge. Score in
squares while warm. Cut when cool and firm. Makes 1 pound of candy.

Fannie Farmer's Chocolate Fudge

2 c sugar
¾ c milk or cream
2 T light corn syrup
4 T cocoa

2 T butter
1 t vanilla
handful of marshmallows (optional)
¾ c chopped pecans

Cook sugar, milk, corn syrup, and cocoa in a heavy saucepan over moderate heat. Stir gently until the chocolate melts, then afterward just enough to keep the fudge from burning. Cook to the softball stage, until a small amount can be formed into a soft ball when dropped into a small glass of water. Remove from heat and add butter, vanilla, marshmallows without stirring.

Let stand until almost cold. Beat with mixer until fudge is no longer glossy and is thick and creamy. Add nuts. Pour into a slightly buttered pan about 8 x 14 in. Makes 1½ pounds.

Frying Pan Fudge

2½ c sugar
1 stick margarine
6 oz evaporated canned milk

6 oz chocolate chips
1 c pecans or other nuts, chopped
1 t vanilla

Mix sugar, margarine and milk in a heavy frying pan and bring to a boil. Reduce heat to low and cook six more minutes, stirring occasionally.

Remove from heat; add chocolate chips and chopped nuts. Stir until fudge begins to form. Then quickly add vanilla and drop fudge on wax paper with teaspoon. Let cool and store in an airtight container.

Cooking is at once child's play and adult joy.
And cooking done with care is an act of love.
— Craig Claiborne

Maple Cream Fudge

2 3-oz pkgs cream cheese
5 c sifted powdered sugar

¼ t maple flavoring
1 c chopped walnuts

Cream cheese until smooth. Slowly blend in powdered sugar. Add maple flavoring and nuts; mix until well blended. Press into a greased 8 x 8 x 2 inch pan. Place in refrigerator until firm. Cut into squares. Better after it sits. Keeps for a month.

Orange Peel Candy ... old recipe from St Leo's Abby

3 large oranges
1½ c sugar, divided

¼ t salt
½ c water

Remove orange peel in quarters; place in saucepan; cover with cold water. Bring to boil; cook until tender, pouring off water and adding fresh cold water several times. Drain peel; cut in thin strips with scissors. Combine 1 cup sugar, salt, and water in saucepan; cook until mixture threads (242 degrees on a candy thermometer). Add peel; cook over low heat until syrup is absorbed. Roll strips in remaining ½ cup sugar until coated. Cool. Makes about ½ pound.

NOTE: 2 teaspoons ground ginger may be combined with ½ cup sugar for coating, if desired.

Microwave Fudge

1 lb box powdered sugar
½ c cocoa
¼ t salt
¼ c milk

1 T vanilla
1 stick margarine
½ c chopped pecans

Place all ingredients except nuts in a mixing bowl. Microwave on high for 2 minutes. Beat with mixer until smooth. Add nuts. Pour into a buttered dish. Can be placed in the freezer, if you are in a hurry.

"Not as good as Fannie Farmer's Fudge, but if you need a chocolate fix in a hurry, this is it."

Research tells us that fourteen out of any ten individuals, like chocolate.
— Sandra Boynton

My Brother Knows Beans

I come from a large family and have many cousins. We all lived within a few blocks of one another when we were children. One evening my brother invited two of his grade-school-aged male cousins, who shall remain nameless here, to spend the night at our house. It was late in the afternoon when they all descended on Mother at suppertime, a not unusual occurrence. That particular evening one of the dishes she'd prepared was her specialty, Boston baked beans prepared southern style, laden with bacon floating in a thick, sweet tomato sauce, one of the family favorites.

As soon as the family and guests were all seated around the table, the youngest of the cousins excitedly said, "Oh boy! Pass me some of those damn beans."

My mother was shocked at such language, and from a tyke. And after a good scolding, my father sent him upstairs to bed without supper.

After a brief period of silence, the other cousin asked, "Could I have some of those damn beans?" Again, my father sent him upstairs to bed.

Then ensued a much longer period of silence. My brother, now alone, an empty chair at each elbow, sat there saying nothing, staring at the wall. Finally, Father asked him, "Don't you want anything to eat?"

"Well, one thing's for sure," my brother said, "I don't want any of them damn beans."

My uncle always said, "Never let the truth stand in the way of a good story."

Ann's Microwave Fudge ... super easy, and good

1 tub of frosting   12 oz chocolate chips
1 c nuts

Melt chocolate chips and frosting in microwave for 2 minutes. Stir until melted, add nuts and pour into a greased pie pan. May cool in refrigerator to harden.

Pecan Cinnamon Fudge ... a fabulous microwave fudge

8½ T butter (not margarine),   ½ c baking cocoa
    divided   1 t cinnamon
¼ c milk   1 c chopped pecans
1½ t vanilla   3 c powdered sugar

Butter a 8-inch square dish with 1 t butter; set aside. In a microwave safe bowl, combine milk and remaining butter. Microwave, uncovered, on high for 1¼ to 1½ minutes or until butter is melted. Stir in vanilla.

In a bowl, combine the powdered sugar, cocoa and cinnamon; stir in milk mixture until blended. Stir in pecans. Pour into prepared pan. Refrigerate for 8 hours or overnight. Cut into squares. Makes 1¼ pounds.

Chocolate is cheaper than therapy and
you don't need an appointment.
— Unknown

Pecan Delights ... chocolate caramel turtles

2¼ c packed brown sugar
1 c butter or margarine
1 c corn syrup
⅛ t salt
1 can sweetened condensed milk

1 t vanilla
1½ pounds whole pecans
1 c milk chocolate chips
1 c semisweet chocolate chips

In a large saucepan: combine the first four ingredients. Cook over medium heat until all the sugar is dissolved. Gradually add milk and mix well. Continue cooking until candy thermometer reads 248 degrees (firm-ball stage.) Remove from the heat; stir in vanilla until blended. Fold in the pecans. Drop by tablespoons onto a greased or parchment-lined cookie sheet. Chill until firm. Loosen from paper. Melt chocolate chips in a microwave-safe bowl. Drizzle over each cluster. Makes about 4 dozen.

Haystacks

¾ c evaporated milk
¾ c lightly packed light brown
  sugar
2 T white corn syrup

¼ c light molasses
2 T butter
3 c shredded coconut

In heavy saucepan, mix the milk, sugar, syrup, molasses and butter. Cook over low heat to boiling point, stirring constantly. Continue cooking, stirring frequently, to 236 degrees on a candy thermometer. Remove from heat and add the coconut gradually. Drop from a tablespoon onto greased pan. Shape into cones with fingers while still warm. Makes about 2 dozen haystacks.

Orange Delight Balls ... wedding cookies in chocolate

1 box vanilla wafers, finely crushed
1 stick butter or margarine, melted
1 lb powdered sugar
6 oz orange juice, thawed

2 c pecans, very finely crushed
12 oz chocolate— Summer coating
  or chocolate chips

Mix vanilla wafers, nuts, powdered sugar and orange juice with melted butter. Mix very well. Form into ¾ inch , walnut size balls. Melt the chocolate in the microwave or in a pan on the stove on the lowest heat. Dip balls and place on waxed paper to harden. Store in airtight container in cool place. Makes 56 balls.

Jessie's Oreo Balls

1 pkg of Oreos
8 oz pkg. Philadelphia Cream Cheese, softened
1+ pkg Wilton White Candy Melts

Crush or Cuisenaire Oreos until big chunks are gone. Mix with Philly cheese until completely mixed. Chill for 3-4 hours if possible. Roll into small balls and dip balls into melted Wilton candy. Cool on waxed paper.

Pecan Christmas Candy

1 c pecans coarsely chopped	1 c cream
1 T butter	2 t vanilla
¼ t cream of tartar	1 c sugar
2 c dark brown sugar	⅛ t salt

Place sugar, butter, vanilla, salt and liquids in a saucepan. Boil while stirring constantly until it forms a soft ball when dropped in ice water. Have greased platter ready. Add the nuts to the candy and the cream of tarter and beat hard until the mixture becomes stiff and creamy. Drop from a tablespoon into cakes on top of the greased platter or waxed paper. Should the mixture harden too quickly, pour into the platter and cut into squares when cool. Wrap each piece separately in wax paper. Will keep for a long time.

This recipe is from a little African-American lady named Alice who lived in the Deep South in 1938 and sold this candy on the streets. This yummy candy is similar to pralines, but has smooth and creamy texture rather than granular.

Jean's Peanut Butter Fudge ... easy and yummee!

2 c sugar	¾ c marshmallow cream
⅔ c evaporated milk	¾ c peanut butter
¼ c margarine	

Boil sugar and milk to softball stage. (230 degrees). Remove from heat and add rest of ingredients. Mix and pour into an 8-9 inch buttered pan.

Spread the table and contention will cease.
— English proverb

Kim's Butterscotch Party Mix ... super!

2 c Chex cereal
2 c small pretzel twists
1 c dry roasted peanuts

20 caramels (quartered)
1 pkg (11 oz) butterscotch chips

Mix the cereal, pretzels, peanuts and caramels. Melt the butterscotch chips in the microwave at 70% for 1 minute. Continue at 10-20 second intervals until smooth. Pour over cereal mixture and pour out on to waxed paper to harden. Once hardened, break apart.

You can sprinkle colorful candies into mixture before it hardens. Red and Green M& M s for Christmas, candy corn for Halloween, pastel M&Ms in the spring...whatever the season. This is so good, I always double Kim's recipe.

Peanut Brittle

2 c sugar
1 c clear corn syrup
¼ c butter

2½ c raw peanuts or other
coarsely chopped nuts
1½ t baking soda, sifted

Butter 2 large cookie sheets; set aside. Butter sides of a heavy 3-quart saucepan. In pan combine sugar, corn syrup, butter, and ½ cup water. Cook and stir over medium-high heat till mixture boils. Place a candy thermometer on saucepan. Lower heat to medium-low; continue boiling at a moderate, steady rate , stirring occasionally, till the thermometer reads 275 degrees, soft crack stage (about 30 minutes). Stir i nuts: continue cooking over medium-low heat, stirring frequently, till thermometer registers 295 degrees, hard crack stage(15-20 minutes).

Remove pan from heat: remove thermometer. Quickly sprinkle baking soda over mixture, stirring constantly. *The candy will foam as the soda reacts chemically with the syrup which makes the brittle porous.* Immediately pour onto prepared cookie sheets. Cool completely; break into pieces. Store tightly covered. Makes 2 ½ pounds.

Peanut Butter Balls ... like a Reese's cup

Small jar of crunchy peanut butter
1 stick margarine, softened
1 lb powdered sugar

chocolate summer coating
or chocolate chips

Mix first 3 ingredients, gradually adding the powdered sugar until dough like consistency. Roll into grape sized balls and dip in summer coating.

Grandma Hughes's Potato Candy ... a family favorite

Cook one medium potato in skin, microwave for 5-7 minutes until soft. Peel and mash in a bowl with a fork. Add powdered sugar until dough like consistency is reached. (About a box) Roll out on waxed paper dusted with more powdered sugar to about ¼ inch thickness. Spread peanut butter on top of "dough" and roll up, jelly roll fashion. Slice.

Very easy and can be made away from the kitchen at church or school with children. I even made this with students recently in China. The Chinese use almost no sugar, and peanut butter was a real treat for them.

Selma's Pralines ... an old Southern Favorite

1½ c brown sugar	1 T butter
1½ c white sugar	1 c water
2 c whole pecan halves	1 t vinegar

Combine sugars, water and vinegar. Cook to softball stage. Add butter and nuts. Remove from heat. Immediately beat until mixture thickens and become cloudy. Quickly drop by heaping tablespoons onto buttered wax paper. Makes 14.

Rollo Pretzel Candy ... quick and good

10 or more tubes of Rollo candy
Bag of mini-pretzels
pecan halves

Line a cookie sheet with Reynolds wrap. Lay as many pretzels in tray as you have individual Rollos. Place a Rollo on top of each pretzel. Warm in a 200 degree oven for 2 minutes. Remove from oven and press each Rollo pretzel with a pecan half. Cool and remove to candy jar.

It's not that chocolates are a substitute for love.
Love is a substitute for chocolate. Chocolate is,
let's face it, far more reliable than a man.
— Miranda Ingram

138

Tiger Butter Candy ... quick and easy

1 lb white chocolate   6 oz chocolate chips
½ c peanut butter

Melt white chocolate in a 2 qt microwave dish for 5 to 8 minutes on 50%
power, stirring every 2 minutes. Stir in peanut butter and spread mixture on
waxed paper on a cookie sheet. Immediately melt chocolate chips in a
microwave on 50% power for 3-5 minutes. Drizzle over peanut butter
layer. With knife or spatula, swirl mixture. Break or cut into pieces.

This is a quick candy to add to the variety of my Christmas candies.

Turtle Bars

½ c white sugar   1 c chopped pecans
½ c white corn syrup   1 t vanilla
¾ c creamy peanut butter   6 oz chocolate chips
3 c Special K cereal   6 oz butterscotch chips

In *large* saucepan, mix together sugar and syrup. Bring to a boil, remove
from heat, and stir in peanut butter. Add cereal, pecans, and vanilla. Stir
together and press into a greased 9 x 13-inch pan. (For thicker bars, use
smaller pan.) Melt chocolate chips and butterscotch chips together on low
heat in pan or in microwave for a minute at a time, until melted. Stir until
smooth. Spread over mixture. When icing hardens cut into squares.

Kate's Strawberry Divinity... pink and yummy

3 c sugar   2 egg white (⅓ c) at room temperature
¾ cup white corn syrup   1 small pkg strawberry Jell-O
¾ c water   1 c chopped pecans

Combine sugar, corn syrup and water in saucepan. Bring to boil, stirring
constantly to dissolve all sugar. Remove remaining sugar crystals from
sides of pan with a damp cloth. Cook to hard boil stage or 252 degrees.
Remove from heat and let stand for a few moments while you prepare egg
whites. Place egg whites in large bowl and beat until foamy. Add Jell-O
and beat until mixture forms soft peaks. Pour hot syrup in a fine, steady
stream while beating constantly. Continue beating until candy loses its
gloss and will hold shape. Fold in pecans and pour into buttered 9 inch
square pan. Cut into squares when cool.

Man cannot live by chocolate alone; but a woman sure can.

Pike County No-Cook Divinity

1 pkg Fluffy white frosting mix
    (dry type)
⅓ c corn syrup
1 t vanilla
½ c boiling water

1 lb powdered sugar
1 c chopped nuts (pecans or
    walnuts)
food coloring

In a small bowl, combine frosting mix, corn syrup, vanilla and water. Beat at high speed with mixer until stiff peaks form. Transfer to large bowl. On low speed, blend in sugar gradually. Food coloring can be added to mixture for seasonal giving. Stir in Chopped nuts. Drop mixture by teaspoon onto waxed paper. When outside of candy feels firm, turn over. Allow to dry overnight. Store in airtight container.

Grandma Hughes's White Fudge

6 c sugar
3 c milk
½ t salt

1 stick butter
2 t vanilla
½ c dates
1 c chopped pecans

Combine sugar, milk and salt, and heat until the soft-ball stage. (Forms a soft ball when dropped into cup of water.) Remove from heat and add butter and vanilla. Cool until 110 degrees or cool enough to handle. *Watch TV for an hour or so.* Beat with a mixer until begins to loose its gloss. Add nuts and dates. Continue to beat by hand until thickened. Pour into a buttered 9 x 12 dish.

Cream Cheese White Chocolate Fudge

8 oz cream cheese, softened   12 oz white chocolate chips
4 c powdered sugar   ¾ c chopped pecans
1½ t vanilla

In a medium bowl, beat cream cheese with mixer. Gradually add in powdered sugar and vanilla and mix until smooth. Melt white chocolate in microwave, making sure not to overcook, by cooking one minute at a time, while stirring. Add melted chocolate to mixture and beat until smooth. Stir in pecans. Pour mixture into a buttered-greased 8 x 8 inch pan. Chill in refrigerator until firm. Cut into small squares.

Never give a dog chocolate, as it contains theobromine (a chemical similar to caffeine) which is a central nervous system stimulant. As little as 2 ounces can be lethal to a small dog.

Appetizers

Apple Dip

8 oz cream cheese, softened
1 c powdered sugar
caramel dip (commercial)

chopped cashews
Gala or favorite apples—cored
  and sliced

Mix cream cheese and powdered sugar and pour into a small cereal bowl lined with saran wrap. Chill. Turn out on plate and place caramel dip on top. Add cashews. Serve with apple slices.

Home-made Caramel Sauce for Apples

Immerse an unopened can of Eagle Brand Milk in a pan of water. Bring to a boil and reduce heat to low. Cook on low for an hour and turn off heat. Cool. When ready to serve, open and pour into serving dish. Serve with Granny Smith Apple slices.

Fruit Cheese Ball ... great

2 8-oz pkg cream cheese
1 small vanilla instant pudding
1 can fruit cocktail, drained

toffee Heath Bits (found in
  chocolate chip section)
lemon snaps or ginger snaps

Mix cream cheese and pudding. Fold in fruit cocktail. Roll in Heath Bits and serve with lemon snaps or ginger snaps.

Fruit Dip ... marvelous

1 small instant vanilla pudding
1¼ c milk

1 small frozen orange juice
¼ c sour cream

Mix and beat pudding, milk, and orange juice for two minutes. Add sour cream and chill. Serve with small pieces of your favorite fruits.

"I come from a family where gravy is considered a beverage."
— Erma Bombeck

Microwave Caramel Corn ... easy and quick

4 quarts popped corn	¼ c corn syrup
1 c brown sugar	½ t salt
¾ stick butter or margarine	½ t soda

Place one large brown paper grocery bag inside another. Put popped corn into the doubled grocery bag. Combine brown sugar, margarine, syrup and salt in a 2-quart deep bowl. Bring to a boil in the microwave (about 2-4 minutes); then cook on high for 2 minutes. Remove from microwave and stir in baking soda. It will foam, thus the large bowl. Mix well and immediately pour syrup over popped corn. Close bag by turning the top down and shake to mix and coat corn.

Cook bag in microwave for 1½ minutes. Remove from microwave and *SHAKE, BABY SHAKE*! Repeat this cooking-shaking process for 2 more times. Pour out onto wax paper, spread, cool, and break apart. Store in closed container.

We usually double this. It is great, easy and quick and the product is always crunchy rather than sticky. Our family has even made this during the half-time of a TV basketball game.

"I prefer butter to margarine, because I trust cows more than I trust chemists."
— Joan Dye Gussow

146

Breakfast

Baked Apple Pancake

1 c pancake mix
⅔ c milk
2 T oil
1 egg, beaten

¼ c margarine
⅓ c packed brown sugar
2 medium apples, peeled and sliced
maple syrup

Combine pancake mix, milk, oil and egg in a large mixing bowl. Melt butter in an 8-inch skillet. Mix in brown sugar and apple slices; sauté until sugar is dissolved. Pour batter over apple mixture. Cook, uncovered, over medium heat until bubbles form on top of pancake. Bake in oven at 350 degrees for 15-20 minutes or until golden brown. Invert on a serving platter. Serve with syrup.

Blueberry Sweet Rolls

1 can blueberry pie filling
8-10 frozen dinner rolls
¾ c brown sugar

1 box instant butterscotch pudding mix
½ c melted butter

Coat a Bundt pan with cooking spray. Pour blueberry pie filling into pan. Space frozen rolls evenly atop pie filling. Sprinkle brown sugar and pudding mix on rolls, let stand at room temperature overnight, so rolls thaw and rise. Drizzle with butter. Bake at 350 degrees until golden brown, about 15 to 20 minutes. Turn out on a serving dish, so blueberry filling is on top.

Cinnamon Jam Biscuits … very easy and good

½ c sugar
½ t cinnamon
¼ c butter or margarine, melted

10 t of your favorite preserves
1 12 oz tube refrigerated buttermilk
    biscuits, separated into 10 biscuits

In a small bowl, combine the sugar and cinnamon. Dip top and sides of biscuits in butter, then in cinnamon-sugar . Place on un-greased baking sheets. With the end of a wooden spoon handle, make a deep indention in the center of each biscuit; fill with 1 teaspoon preserves.

Bake at 375 degrees for 15-18 minutes or until golden brown. Cool for 15 minutes before serving. Serves 10

Blueberry Nut Bread

1 pt blueberries, rinsed but not dried	1 c oil
3 c plus 3 T flour, divided	4 eggs
2 c sugar	1 t baking soda
1 c chopped nuts	1 t ground cinnamon
	1 t salt

Preheat the oven to 350 degrees and coat two 9 x 5 loaf pans with Pam. In a medium bowl, combine the damp blueberries and 3 T flour; toss to coat evenly. In a large bowl, combine the remaining ingredients and mix well. Carefully stir in the coated blueberries, and then spoon the mixture into two loaf pans. Bake 55-60 minutes or until a wooden tooth pick inserted in the center comes out clean. Allow to cool slightly, and then remove to a wire rack to cool completely. Serve with cream cheese.

Brown Sugar Cream Cheese Muffins

½ c brown sugar, firmly packed	1 c old fashioned oats, uncooked
⅓ c margarine, softened	½ c flour
3 oz cream cheese, softened	⅓ c whole wheat flour
⅔ c milk	1 T baking powder
1 large egg	½ t salt
1 t maple or vanilla extract	1 c chopped pecans, divided

Grease only the bottoms of 12 muffin cups or line with paper baking cups. In a medium bowl, beat the brown sugar, margarine and cream cheese with a mixer until light and fluffy. Add the milk, egg and extract, mixing well. In another bowl, combine the oats, both flours, baking powder and salt; whisk to combine. Add this and ½ cup pecans to the sugar-butter mixture, stirring just until the dry ingredients are moistened. Spoon the batter into the muffin cups, filling each three-quarters full. Sprinkle the remaining pecans over the tops. Bake at 400 degree for 18-22 minutes, or until the muffins are golden brown. Freezes well.

My mother's menu consisted of two choices: Take it or leave it.
— Buddy Hackett

150

Cranberry Coffee Cake

Cake:
2 c biscuit mix
2 T sugar
⅔ c milk
1 egg, beaten
⅔ c jellied cranberry sauce

Topping:
½ c chopped walnuts
½ c packed brown sugar
½ t cinnamon
Glaze:
1 c powdered sugar
2 T milk
¼ t vanilla

In a large bow, combine the biscuit mix, sugar milk and egg. Pour into a greased 8 inch square baking dish. Drop cranberry sauce by teaspoonfuls over batter. Combine topping ingredients; sprinkle over cranberry sauce. Bake at 400 degrees for 18 - 23 minutes or until a toothpick inserted near the center comes out clean. Cool on a wire rack. In a small bowl, combine the glaze ingredients; drizzle over coffee cake. Serves 9.

Christmas Morning Cranberry Casserole ... yummy

3 c chopped apples
2 c fresh cranberries
2 T flour
1 c sugar
3 1⅝-oz pkg. instant oatmeal
    with cinnamon

¾ c chopped pecans
½ c flour
½ c brown sugar
½ c margarine
additional cranberries and
    pecans for topping

Combine apples, cranberries and flour, tossing to coat. Add 1 cup sugar, mixing well. Place in a 2 qt casserole dish. Combine oatmeal, chopped pecans, ½ c flour and brown sugar; add butter and stir well. Spoon over fruit mixture. Bake uncovered at 350 degree for 45 minutes. Garnish with cranberries and pecan pieces before baking.

An onion can make people cry, but there has never been
a vegetable invented to make them laugh.
— Will Rogers

151

French Toast

2 eggs
¼ c sugar
½ t cinnamon

½ c milk
4 or 5 slices bread

Beat eggs, then beat in the sugar and the milk and cinnamon. Soak the bread slices in mixture and fry in a skillet with margarine.

Stuffed French Toast

8 slices sourdough bread
2 bananas
½ c sugar
1 t cinnamon

2 eggs
½ c milk
1 t vanilla

Cut bananas lengthwise, and then crosswise to get about 8 pieces flat on one side. Cut pockets in each piece of bread, insert a banana slice in each. Mix sugar and cinnamon and set aside. Mix eggs, milk and vanilla in shallow dish. Soak sandwiches, turning once, about 6 minutes. Heat oil in large saucepan or skillet to 350 degrees. Add sandwiches, sauté until golden brown, place on paper towels and sprinkle with cinnamon sugar.

Lemon Pull-Apart Coffee Cake

12 Rhodes Dinner Rolls, thawed,
    but still cold
2 lemon rinds, grated
½ c sugar
¼ c melted butter

Citrus Glaze:
1 c powdered sugar
1 T butter, melted
2 T fresh lemon juice

Mix grated lemon rind with sugar. Cut rolls in half and place in a 12-inch deep dish pizza pan or 9 x 13 inch baking pan sprayed with a non-stick cooking spray. Drizzle ¼ cup melted butter over rolls. Sprinkle with lemon rind/sugar mixture, reserving ½ of mixture to sprinkle on just before baking. Cover with plastic wrap.

Let rise until double in size. Remove wrap. Sprinkle on remaining mixture. Bake at 350 degrees for 20-25 minutes. Remove immediately from pan and place on cooling rack. Combine powdered sugar, butter and lemon juice. Mix well. Drizzle glaze over the pull-aparts.

Orange Breakfast Ring

1 c sugar
3 T grated orange rind
2 12-oz cans biscuits
½ c margarine

3 oz cream cheese, softened
½ c powdered sugar
2 T orange juice

Combine sugar and orange rind. Separate biscuits; dip each in butter and coat with sugar mixture. Stand biscuits on edges in a 9-inch tube pan and bake at 350 degrees for 30 minutes or until brown. Invert on serving plate and remove ring from pan. Combine cream cheese and powdered sugar. Add juice, stirring well. Spoon over top of breakfast ring. Serve warm.

Plum Cake

Mix together:
2 c sugar
1 c oil
Add:
3 eggs, one at a time, beating well
2 t red food coloring
2 small baby food jars of plums
    with tapioca

Sift together:
2 c flour
½ t soda
1 t nutmeg
1 t cinnamon
½ t salt
1 c broken pecans or walnuts

Sift dry ingredients into liquid mixture. Add nuts. Bake in 2 loaf pans or 1 bundt pan for 1 hour at 325 degrees. Mix 1 cup powdered sugar and 3 T orange juice and drizzle over warm cake.

Chocolate syrup was used for the blood in the famous shower scene in the Alfred Hitchcock movie *'Psycho'*. The scene lasts for about 45 seconds in the movie, but took 7 days to film.

Raspberry-Cheese Coffee Cake

8 oz cream cheese, softened
½ c butter, softened
1 c sugar
2 large eggs
¼ c milk
½ t vanilla

1¾ cups flour
1 t baking powder
½ t baking soda
¼ t salt
½ cups raspberry preserves
3 T powdered sugar, for garnish

Beat first 3 ingredients at medium speed until creamy. Combine eggs, milk, and vanilla, beating until smooth. Add while mixing, flour and next 3 ingredients to cream cheese mixture. Beat at slow speed until well blended. Pour batter into a greased and floured 9 x 13 pan. Dollop with preserves and swirl. Bake at 350 degrees for 30 minutes or until cake begins to shrink from sides of pan. Cool; sprinkle with powdered sugar.

Sticky Buns

24 frozen white dinner roll dough balls
1 small cook and serve
   butterscotch pudding
½ c butter

¾ t cinnamon
¾ c brown sugar
½ c chopped nuts

Spray a bundt pan well with Pam. Sprinkle nuts evenly in bottom of pan. Place frozen dough balls on top of nuts. Sprinkle dry pudding over dough balls. In small saucepan, melt butter. Add cinnamon and brown sugar and allow to simmer for five minutes. Pour over dough balls. Cover with a greased, light piece of foil and allow to sit overnight on counter to rise. Bake uncovered at 350 degrees for 15 minutes, then cover with foil (to prevent browning) and bake another 15 minutes. Let stand for 5 minutes and then invert on a serving plate.

Marmalade Sticky Buns ... easy and quick

⅔ cup orange marmalade
½ c chopped pecans or walnuts
¼ c honey

2 T butter, melted
2 (7 ½ oz) tubes refrigerated
  buttermilk biscuits

In a small bowl, combine the marmalade, pecans, honey and butter. Cut each biscuit into four pieces. Layer half of the pecans in a greased bundt pan; top with half of the marmalade mixture. Repeat. Bake at 375 degrees for 27-30 minutes or until golden brown. Cool in pan for 5 minutes before inverting onto a serving plate. Serve warm. Serves 8.

Inez's Sour Cream Coffee Cake ... rich and good

1 c sour cream
¾ t soda
1 c margarine
1 c sugar

2 eggs
1 t vanilla
1 ½ c flour, sifted
1 ½ t baking powder

Note: Mix sour cream and soda together and let stand one hour.

Cream margarine and sugar, add eggs and sour cream and vanilla. Sift flour and baking powder together and mix into other ingredients. Beat well.

Filling/Topping:

½ c brown sugar
1 t cinnamon

1 c chopped nuts

Put half cake batter in greased 9 inch square or 7 x 12 inch pyrex dish. Sprinkle half or more of filling over it. Top with remaining batter then sprinkle remainder of topping over it. Bake 40 minutes at 350 degrees.

Ask not what you can do for your country. Ask what's for lunch.
— Orson Welles

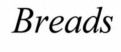

Breads

Tart Apple Muffins

Muffins:
1 pkg apple cinnamon muffin mix
1 large apple, peeled and diced
⅓ c chopped nuts
3 T brown sugar
5 t flour
1 T margarine, melted

Glaze:
1 c powdered sugar
1 t vanilla
2 T milk

Prepare muffin mix; fold in apples. Fill 6 greased muffins cups ¾ full. Combine nuts, brown sugar, flour and butter; drizzle over batter. Bake at 400 degrees for 15-20 minutes or until lightly browned. Cool for a few minutes, remove from pan. Combine glaze and drizzle over warm muffins.

Banana Bread ... a special old family recipe

1 c sugar
½ c shortening
3 large bananas, mashed
2 eggs
2 c flour

½ c nuts
1 t soda in 2 T water
½ t salt
1 t vanilla

Cream sugar and shortening. Add eggs. Add remaining ingredients. Bake in a greased loaf pan at 375 degrees for 50 minutes.

What you see before you, my friend, is the result of a lifetime of chocolate.
— Katharine Hepburn, who lived to the age of 96.

Orange Date Nut Bread

1 large orange	1 beaten egg
1 c pitted dates, chopped	2 c sifted flour
1 t soda	1 t baking powder
⅔ c sugar	¼ t salt
2 T butter	½ c nuts
1 t vanilla	

Squeeze juice from the orange into a measuring cup. Add boiling water to make 1 cup liquid. Put orange rind through food chopper and add enough chopped dates to equal 1 cup. Place into mixing bowl. Add juice. Stir in soda, sugar, butter and vanilla. Add beaten egg, then flour which has been sifted with baking powder and salt. Add nuts. Place in pan greased with shortening and floured. Bake in pre-heated oven for 50 minutes at 350 degrees in 2 small or 1 long loaf pan. Cool. Slice thin and spread with a mixture of cream cheese, crushed pineapple and flaked coconut.

Pumpkin Bread

2 cups sugar	2 t salt
1 c oil	1 t baking powder
4 beaten eggs	1 t nutmeg
1 16-oz can pumpkin	1 t allspice
3½ c flour	1 t cinnamon
2 t soda	½ t cloves
⅔ c water	optional: coconut raisins, nuts

Combine and mix oil, eggs and pumpkin. Add and mix flour, soda, salt, baking powder, spices and water. Add raisins, coconut and nuts. Bake at 350 degrees for 1½ hours. Makes 2 loaves.

'I'm like old wine. They don't bring me out
very often, but I'm well preserved."
— Rose Kennedy, on her 100 birthday.

Salads

—

Sweet enough for dessert, if you'd like.

Ambrosia ... a dessert or a salad

Oranges
20 oz crushed pineapple

1 pkg frozen crushed coconut
Kool Whip (optional)

Peel the oranges and separate the sections. Peel and seed the sections over a large bowl, so as not to lose any juice. Add pineapple, coconut and a little sugar to taste. Mix well and taste to see if sweet enough. Keep in refrigerator until ready to use. Top with Kool Whip if desired.

Bing Cherry Salad

2 pkg cherry flavored Jell-O
2½ c cherry juice (1 can with liquid)
1 c port wine

1 c chopped pecans
1 c Bing cherries
1 8-oz pkg cream cheese

Dissolve Jell-O in the heated cherry juice and water. Cool and when Jell-O has begun to congeal, add the wine, nuts and cherries. Chill until set.

Topping:
Soften 1 pkg cream cheese with port wine and spread over the top.

Frosted Blueberry Salad

1 15-oz can blueberries
1 6 oz pkg sugar free raspberry Jell-O
2 c boiling water
½ c fat free sour cream
½ t vanilla

1 8-oz can unsweetened pineapple tidbits
8 oz cream cheese, softened
⅓ c sugar

Drain blueberries and pineapple. Reserve juice, set fruit aside. In bowl dissolve Jell-O in boiling water. Add enough water to juice to make 1½ cup. Stir into Jell-O. Chill in a flat dish until partially set. Stir in fruit and refrigerate. In mixing bowl combine cream cheese and sour cream. Beat in sugar and vanilla. Spread over Jell-O and refrigerate.

A balanced diet is a cookie in each hand.
— Kathy Brussell

Blueberry Pie Salad

2 small boxes grape Jell-O
2 c boiling water
1 can crushed pineapple, drained
1 can blueberry pie filling

½ c sugar
½ pint sour cream
8 oz cream cheese
1 t vanilla

Mix jell-o with boiling water. Add pineapple and pie filling and refrigerate overnight. Combine sugar, sour cream, cream cheese and vanilla and beat. Spread over jell-o mixture.

Cherry Pie Salad

1 can Eagle Brand condensed milk
1 large container Kool Whip
1 can cherry pie filling

1 can crushed pineapple
½ c nuts, chopped

Blend milk and Kool Whip. Add pie filling and drained pineapple and nuts. Chill.

Coca-Cola Salad

½ c sugar
½ c water
1 c Coca-Cola or Pepsi
1 can dark sweet cherries, pitted

2 small boxes cherry Jell-O
1 small can crushed pineapple
½ c chopped pecans

Mix water, sugar and juices from cherries and pineapple. Boil five minutes. Dissolve Jell-O in the hot mixture and add Coke or Pepsi. Add the nuts and cherries and mix well. Place in the refrigerator until congealed.

Cranberry Congealed Salad … holiday favorite

1 pkg plain Knox gelatin
    dissolved in ½ c cold water
1 large black raspberry Jell-O
2 c boiling water

1 can crushed pineapple, with juice
1 can cranberry sauce with berries
1 carton sour cream

Dissolve Jell-O in boiling water and add gelatin. Add pineapple with juice. Stir cranberry sauce in can to mix and then add to Jell-O mixture. Pour into 9x13 pan and refrigerate about 1 hour. Stir sour cream and spread on top or swirl into salad.

Frozen Cranberry Banana Salad

1 20-oz can pineapple tidbits
5 medium firm bananas,
    halved lengthwise & sliced
16 oz whole berry cranberry sauce
¼ c sugar
12 oz Kool Whip, thawed
½ c chopped nuts

Drain pineapple juice into a medium bowl and set aside. Add sliced bananas to the juice. In large bowl, combine cranberry sauce and sugar. Remove bananas from juice and discard the juice. Add the bananas to the cranberry mixture. Stir in pineapple, Kool Whip and nuts. Pour into a 13x9 dish and freeze. Serves twelve to sixteen.

Frozen Cranberry Banana Salad … made simple

1 can whole cranberries
1 can crushed pineapple
1 small box cranberry Jell-O
½ c nuts

Mix pineapple and gelatin together in saucepan and let it come to a boil. Remove from heat, add cranberries and nuts. Pour into a mold.

Cranberry Delight … one of my favorites

12 oz fresh cranberries
1 c English walnuts, chopped
1 lb grapes, halved and seeded
1 c sugar
1 small container Kool Whip

Grind cranberries coarsely in food chopper or blender. Add sugar and mix until dissolved. Let stand in refrigerator overnight. The next day, drain for about four hours. Meanwhile, prepare the nuts and grapes. When cranberries have drained, add nuts, grapes and Kool Whip and blend well. Chill thoroughly. Serves six to eight.

My family loves this salad, and it is one of my traditional Christmas dinner salads.

Can it be a mistake that STRESSED is DESSERTS spelled backwards?
— Karen Campbell

Curried Fruit

1 large can peach halves
1 medium can pear halves
1 medium can pineapple chunks
¾ c brown sugar
⅓ c melted butter

1 T curry powder
½ c blanched slivered almonds
1 small jar maraschino cherries

Drain fruit thoroughly. Spread all except cherries in shallow baking dish. Put a cherry in each pear and peach half. Sprinkle almonds over all. Combine brown sugar, melted butter and the curry powder and top fruit with the mixture. Bake at 325 degrees for 1½ hours. Serves six.

Five Cup Salad ... an old family favorite

1 c pineapple, drained
1 c mandarin oranges, drained
1 c tiny marshmallows

1 c shredded coconut
1 c sour cream

Mix and chill, if possible. May double or triple ingredients.

Fruit Delight ... easy and good

1 large can chunk pineapple,
   drained
1 can mandarin oranges, drained
⅓ c lemon juice
½ c orange juice

1 T cornstarch
½ c sugar or sweetener
4-5 apples, chopped
4-5 bananas chopped

Mix juice of pineapple and oranges with lemon and orange juices. Add cornstarch and sugar. Heat until boiling. Cool and pour over fruit. *Salad will keep for days in refrigerator; the juices keep the bananas from turning brown.*

I have this theory that chocolate slows down the aging process....
It may not be true, but do I dare take the chance?
— Unknown

Fruit Salad

1 small box vanilla pudding
1 can pineapple tidbits, drained
1 can mandarin oranges, drained
1-2 c white grapes

1 c Kool Whip
1 c mini marshmallows
1 c chopped nuts

Cook pudding with 1½ c of the juice from the fruits instead of milk. Cool. Add Kool Whip, fruit, nuts and marshmallows

Four Layer Salad ... a.k.a. Sawdust Salad

First layer:

1 pkg orange Jell-O
1 pkg lemon Jell-O
2 c hot water
1½ c cold water

2 large bananas
1 #2 can crushed pineapple, drained
mini marshmallows as needed

Dissolve Jell-O in hot water. Add cold water. Add drained pineapple, sliced bananas. Pour into 9 x 13 x 2 pan. Cover with little marshmallows and place in refrigerator to set.

Second layer:

1 c pineapple juice
1 whole egg

½ c sugar
2 T flour

Combine pineapple juice, egg, and sugar and flour and place into a small saucepan. Cook, stirring constantly over medium heat until thick. Let cool. Spread over first layer.

Third layer:

1 pkg Kool Whip   8 oz soft cream cheese

Mix Kool Whip, and cream cheese until smooth. Spread over second layer.

Fourth layer:

Grated cheddar cheese
Cover the salad with cheese and chill.

The trouble with eating Italian food is that five or six days later, you're hungry again.
— George Miller

Green Salad ... an old family favorite

1 #2 can crushed pineapple
1 pkg lime Jell-O
1 pkg lemon Jell-O
2 c boiling water
2 c cottage cheese

1 c pineapple juice(juice from can
    plus water to make a cup)
¾ c salad dressing
⅓ c chopped pecans
salt

Drain pineapple. Dissolve Jell-O in hot water. Add pineapple juice. Add salad dressing and blend with mixer. Pour into flat pans and chill in freezer 15-20 minutes until it thickens around the edges. Turn into mixer and whip until fluffy. Fold in pineapple, cottage cheese and pecans. Chill until firm.

Green Cherry Salad

1 small pkg lime Jell-O
1 c boiling water
1 c Pet Milk
16 oz crushed pineapple
⅓ c maraschino cherries

¼ c celery
¼ c English walnuts
½ c mayonnaise
1 c cottage cheese

Dissolve Jell-O in boiling water. Cool to room temperature. Add remaining ingredients and mix. Chill in serving dish in refrigerator. Top with cherries.

Mandarin Orange Salad I

1 small cottage cheese
1 box orange Jell-O
1 small can mandarin oranges

1 small can crushed pineapple
1 small Kool Whip

Mix cottage cheese and Jell-O powder. Drain oranges and pineapple and add to Jell-O and cottage cheese. Mix in Kool Whip and refrigerate overnight.

When opening canned goods, open the end that had been sitting on the shelf. The ingredients come out more easily, and that end is usually cleaner.

Injustice anywhere is a threat to justice everywhere.
— Martin Luther King, from the Birmingham Jail

Mandarin Orange Salad II

1 large pkg lemon Jell-O
2 c hot water
1 large can mandarin oranges

1 medium can crushed pineapple
1 c miniature marshmallows
2 bananas

Drain oranges and pineapple and reserve juice. Dissolve Jell-O in hot water and add 1½ cups cold orange juice or water. Add orange sections, pineapple, marshmallows, and the partially mashed bananas. Let set up in refrigerator and cover with topping.

Topping
½ c pineapple juice
2 T flour
½ c sugar

1 egg
2 T butter

Cook and stir until thick then add 3 oz. cream cheese, cool and add one package of dream whip. Mix and spread over Jell-O.

Mandarin Orange Salad III

60 Ritz Crackers, finely crushed
¼ lb margarine, melted
¼ c sugar
1 6-oz can unsweetened frozen
    orange juice
1 can sweetened condensed milk

8 oz Kool Whip
2 small cans mandarin oranges,
    drained
1 can crushed pineapple, drained
optional: ½ bottle maraschino cherries

Mix crackers crumbs, butter and sugar. Press mixture firmly into a 9 x 13 baking dish, reserving some crumbs for garnish. Blend thawed orange juice with milk. Fold in Kool whip, oranges, pineapple, and cherries. Do not beat. Pour mixture over crust. Top with reserved crumbs. Refrigerate or freeze until saving.

There's nothing better than a good friend, except a good friend with chocolate.
— *Linda Grayson, "The Pickwick Papers"*

Orange Delight

2 c water
3 oz orange Jell-O
15 oz mandarin oranges, drained
4 oz Kool Whip

small instant vanilla pudding
small instant tapioca pudding
15 oz crushed pineapple, drained

Bring water to boil. Whisk in gelatin and pudding mixes. Return to boil, stirring constantly. Remove from heat and cool. Fold in oranges and pineapple and Kool Whip. Spoon into serving bowl. Cool 2 hours.

Topping for Jell-O Salads

1 pkg instant lemon pudding
1 c milk
½ pt whipping cream

Beat pudding mix with milk until slightly firm. Whip cream and fold into pudding. Spread on gelatin.

Peach Pie Fruit Salad

2 qt strawberries, diced
4-5 bananas
1 can mandarin oranges, drained

1 can pineapple chunks or tidbits, drained
1 can peach pie filling

Mix all ingredients and refrigerate.

Pistachio Salad ... an old, quick goodie

3½ oz instant pistachio
    pudding mix
8 oz crushed pineapple,

1 large Kool Whip
½ c chopped nuts
1 c miniature marshmallows

Mix together and refrigerate. Best if refrigerated overnight.

Mom Hughes's Lime Pickles … sweetest pickle ever

7 lbs cucumbers	2 c pickling lime
(about 4" long)	2 gal water

Cut cucumbers in slices and soak in a crock container, not a plastic container, with pickling lime and water for 24 hours. Mixture will separate and should be mixed by hand 3-4 times. After 24 hours rinse several times in cool clear water and soak in cool water for 3 hours. Mix the following in a large cooking pot:

2 qt vinegar	1 t mixed pickling spice
4½ lbs sugar (9 cups)	½ T salt

Put pickles in pot and simmer for 35 minutes and put in clean mason jars (dishwasher cleaning is adequate). Boil lids and rings. Fill jars to top with pickles and hot vinegar solution. Place rings around lids and tighten down. Let cool upside down for 10 minutes, turn right side up and jars will seal.

These are the best sweet pickles you will ever eat. My friend, Stephen Holthaus, was moved to praise these pickles in song.

I don't want a pickle
Jus' wanna ride my motor-sickle

And I don't wanna die
Jus' wanna ride my motor-sie

But that's all changed since I ate your pickles
Don't really care about them motor-sickles

Don't really care even if I die
long as I have one of them pickles 'fore I say goodbye

— With apologies from Stephen Holthaus to Arlo Guthrie.

The Three Musketeers candy bar was introduced in 1932.
The original had 3 bars in one wrapper,
each with a different flavor.

Pineapple Slaw ... I really like this.

2-3 c shredded cabbage
   (bagged slaw is fine)
1-2 T milk
2 T vinegar

1 8-oz can pineapple tidbits, drained
2 T sugar
½ c mayonnaise or salad dressing

Combine mayonnaise, vinegar, sugar and milk. Place cabbage and pineapple in a large bowl; add dressing and toss.

Pineapple-Nut Salad

1 can crushed pineapple
½ c pecans
½ c cherries

8 oz Kool Whip
8 oz cream cheese
2 T sugar or substitute

Beat cream cheese with juice from pineapple until smooth and fluffy. Stir in remaining ingredients.

For several years I've been getting this tasty salad off the Kroger salad bar. I think I've finally figured out how to make it.

Cherry Salad

1 can cherry pie filling
1 can crushed pineapple
   (drained)
¼ c lemon juice

can sweetened condensed milk
¼ t vanilla
2 c Cool Whip

Mix all ingredients together except Kool Whip; then fold in Kool Whip. Chill.

"Give me liberty or ...OOOooo.. A jelly donut!
— Homer Simpson

Red, White, & Blue Salad

2 3-oz pkg Raspberry Jell-O
3 c hot water
1 envelope plain gelatin
½ c cold water
1 c sugar

1 t vanilla
1 8-oz pkg cream cheese
1 c coffee cream
½ c chopped nuts
1 #303 can blueberries and juice

First layer:
1 pkg raspberry Jell-O dissolved in 2 c hot water. Pour into an 8 x 12 pan and let set.

Second layer:
Soften plain gelatin in cold water. Heat on low, heat the coffee cream with sugar; combine with gelatin. Add vanilla, softened cream cheese and chopped nuts. Put on top of first layer.

Third layer:
After second layer is firm, combine 1 pkg raspberry gelatin with 1-cup hot water and add blueberries, juice and all. Put on top of second layer. Put in refrigerator until firm.

Strawberry Pretzel Salad ... very good & crunchy

2 c thin pretzels, broken
    into small pieces
1 stick butter melted
4 T sugar & 1 c sugar
8 oz Kool Whip, thawed
8 oz cream cheese

6 oz strawberry Jell-O
2 cups boiling water
½ c cold water
16 oz frozen strawberries

Crust:
Combine pretzels, margarine and 4 tablespoons sugar. Pat into a greased 9 x 13 pan. Bake at 325 degrees for 10 minutes. Let cool.

First Layer;
Make middle layer by combining Kool Whip with cream cheese and 1 cup sugar. Pour into cooled crust.

Top Layer:
Combine Jell-O with water and strawberries. When thick, pour on top of cream cheese layer. Chill until set.

Strawberry Cream Squares ... a special family favorite

2 3-oz pkgs strawberry Jell-O
2 c boiling water
2 10-oz pkgs frozen strawberries
1 13½-oz can crushed pineapple
2 large bananas
1-2 c sour cream

Dissolve Jell-O in boiling water. Add frozen strawberries, and stir occasionally till thawed. Add pineapple and bananas, finely chopped. Pour half into 9 x 13 x 2 pan or a large clear bowl. Chill until firm. Spread evenly with sour cream. Cover with remainder of Jell-O mixture. Chill.

Strawberry Party Salad

3 oz strawberry Jell-O
1 can crushed pineapple,
   drained(save juice)
1 pound cottage cheese
1 medium Kool whip
nuts, optional

Heat the juice and jell-o and mix. Add pineapple and boil one minute. Cool. Add the cottage cheese and Kool whip. Add nuts if desired. Chill in the refrigerator. Serves: 6.

Easy Strawberry Salad

8 oz cottage cheese
3½ oz box of sugar-free strawberry
   Jell-o
11 oz crushed pineapple
11 oz mandarin oranges
8 oz Kool Whip

Mix cottage cheese and Jell-o. Drain fruit and add to Jell-o mixture. Add Kool Whip. Cool in refrigerator.

Weightless Fruit Salad

1 can of fruit cocktail, light
1 can of pineapple tidbits, light
1 can of pears, light
1 small pkg of fat-free, sugar-
   free vanilla pudding

Use same size cans of fruit; drain and mix together. Pour dry pudding on top and mix well. Refrigerate overnight. Just before serving may add fresh bananas, strawberries or blueberries.

I often add to this easy combination whatever fruit I have on hand.

White Salad

2 pkgs unflavored gelatin
¼ c cold water
1 8-oz pkg cream cheese
⅔ c chopped walnuts

1 large can crushed pineapple
1 c sugar
1 c of Kool Whip

Boil sugar and pineapple mixture for 5 minutes. Dissolve gelatin in cold water and stir into pineapple mixture. Chill until the consistency of unbeaten egg whites. Soften cream cheese and whip until smooth. Add chopped walnuts. Fold in Kool Whip. Refrigerate.

The two biggest sellers in bookstores are the cookbooks and the diet books. The cookbooks tell you how to prepare the food and the diet books tell you how not to eat any of it.
— Andy Rooney

Fruits & Vegetables

—

Other unusual sweet stuff —

In the South we'll put sugar in anything.

Really Sweet Baked Beans ... the quick and easy way

1 can baked beans, drained

4 T butter
1 c brown sugar
¼ c ketchup

2 T Worcestershire sauce
3 T dried onions
4 bacon strips, cut in small pieces

Melt butter and brown sugar in sauce pan. Cook for a few minutes until thickened. Add ketchup, Worcestershire sauce, onions and bacon. Cook until thickened and bacon is done. Add beans and heat until all is warmed. A friend who gave me this recipe told me that he used it when he was a cook in the army. Now it's my usual way of preparing baked beans, especially when I'm pressed for time, or the oven is full of other dishes.

Cranberry and Apple Bake

2 c uncooked cranberries
3 c peeled and chopped apples
2 c brown sugar, divided

7 T margarine, melted
1 c quick cooking oatmeal

Stir the cranberries, apples and 1 cup of sugar in a mixing bowl. Melt margarine in a medium saucepan; add oatmeal and remaining cup of sugar and mix well. Pour the apple mixture into a greased baking dish. Top with the oatmeal mixture. Bake at 350 degrees for 1 hour.

Pineapple Casserole ... easy and simply marvelous

2 cans chunk pineapple, (drained)

1 c sugar
¼ c flour

2 rolls Ritz crackers, crushed
2 sticks butter, melted

Mix pineapple, sugar and flour, and place in baking dish. Mix crackers and butter, and place on top of pineapple mixture. Bake 30-40 minutes at 350 degrees.

Don't agonize, organize!
— Lee Smith

179

Pineapple Beans

28-oz can baked beans
8-oz can pineapple tidbits, drained
4½ oz jar sliced mushrooms,
    drained
1 large red or green bell pepper,
    chopped

1 large onion, chopped fine
½ c smoked barbeque sauce
2 T soy sauce
2 cloves garlic, chopped fine
½ t salt
¼ t black pepper

Place all ingredients in a crock pot. Cover and cook on low 4-8 hours.
Serves 8-10.

Sweet Barbequed Green Beans

1 16-oz can green beans
1 large onion, diced
3 slices bacon, cut up

½ c ketchup
¼ c vinegar
½ c sugar

Brown bacon and onions. Add ketchup, vinegar and sugar. Simmer until slightly thick. Drain beans and put in casserole dish. Pour sauce over beans. Mix and bake at 325 degrees about 30 minutes.

Easy, and a really fantastic dish with any chicken or special dinner. Like I said— In the South we'll put sugar in anything.

Life expectancy would grow by leaps and bounds if
green vegetables smelled as good as bacon.
— Doug Larson

Fried Green Beans … unique, but good

3 medium size cans of green beans
½ cup sugar (may add more if desired)
5 strips of bacon fried crisp

Fry bacon until very crisp in heavy large skillet and crumble into small pieces. Put green beans and half of sugar into bacon grease and fry beans on medium heat stirring occasionally. Continue adding sugar until all is gone and continue frying beans while stirring occasionally until beans cook down. Add crumbled bacon shortly before taking beans up to serve.

Raisin Sauce For Ham

Mix:	*Add:*
½ c brown sugar	¼ c vinegar
½ T mustard	1¾ c water
2 heaping T flour	½ c raisins

Place in saucepan and cook until thick over medium heat. Add raisins. Serve over sliced ham.

If it looks like a duck, walks like a duck, talks like a duck,
it probably needs a little more time in the microwave.
— Lori Dowdy

LaVergne, TN USA
14 October 2010
200800LV00003B/2/A